Education and Politics in Suburbia:
The New Trier Experience

# EDUCATION AND POLITICS IN SUBURBIA

## The New Trier Experience

*By*
*Louis H. Masotti*

Cleveland
THE PRESS OF
WESTERN RESERVE UNIVERSITY
1967

*For Iris and Laura Lynn*

# Preface

In May, 1961, the voters of suburban Chicago's New Trier Township High School District rejected the Board of Education's proposal to build a second four-year school in the district. The defeat of this referendum was notable for two reasons. It was the first major referendum defeat (and only the second defeat) in the sixty-three-year history of New Trier's nationally respected school system. Perhaps more significant was the fact that this defeat offered tangible evidence of the social conflict that had been developing within the community during the preceding decade.

To a community where local elections are *pro forma* exercises in the legitimation of decisions made by hired experts (city managers and school superintendents), and where avoidance of controversy is the norm, the 1961 referendum was unsettling. Subsequent events have resolved the expansion controversy to the apparent satisfaction of almost all concerned. But for a period of several years, at least, there was considerable concern about the implications of this dispute for the future tranquillity of the New Trier community.

In this volume, the conditions that generated the New Trier expansion conflict and the events that led to its resolution are described and analyzed. The aim is to show how public education becomes increasingly politicized in the suburbs, as these areas—where schools and education provide an important focus of community life—respond to the challenges of dynamic change.

The author wishes to acknowledge the considerable debt he owes to the many people who contributed to this book. The numerous public officials and private citizens of the New Trier Township High School District gave generously of their time and patience for over a year. The faculty of the Department of Political Science, Northwestern University, and especially David W.

Minar, helped to formulate the original project and offered incisive and constructive criticism throughout. I am grateful to the Center for Metropolitan Studies of Northwestern University for financial assistance while the first draft was being researched and written. The staff at The Press of Western Reserve University was extremely helpful in making the book readable. I can only inadequately express my gratitude to my wife, who typed and edited several versions of the manuscript, while simultaneously serving as housewife and mother. All of these people deserve credit for making this book possible, but I take personal responsibility for any errors of fact or interpretation.

# Table of Contents

# List of Illustrations

# List of Tables

Education and Politics in Suburbia:
The New Trier Experience

# 1 | A Profile of the New Trier Community

New Trier Township High School in suburban Chicago is ranked by professional educators among the very best secondary public school systems in the nation, along with the secondary schools of Scarsdale and Great Neck, New York, Newton, Massachusetts, and Shaker Heights, Ohio, Philadelphia's Central High School, and the Bronx High School of Science. James B. Conant, the "inspector-general" of education under the aegis of the Carnegie Foundation and the Education Testing Service, refers to such schools as "lighthouse" schools—"beacons lighting the way toward educational progress":

> There can be no doubt of the excellence of the teaching in the lighthouse school districts. Large school budgets enable the superintendent and the principals of the schools to recruit a corps of first-rate teachers; the level of the salaries is far higher than in many other districts. Furthermore the size of the staff is as much as 75 per cent greater than the corresponding schools in the nearby large central city. Physical facilities are usually the envy of those who live in less prosperous school districts. In short, the high costs per pupil are an essential factor in assuring the excellence of these schools.
>
> Yet it could be a mistake to assume that the high expenditures are the only factor. In addition to a top-flight teaching staff, the lighthouse schools are fortunate in the nature of the student body. The vast majority of the pupils come from homes that are by no means typical in the United States. The attitude of the parents toward education, toward music, art, drama, literature and politics is far different from that of the average American family. Most of the fathers and many of the

mothers are college graduates. Shall we say that the cultural level and the degree of social sophistication are extremely high?[1]

## The New Trier Township High School District

By these and other criteria, New Trier seems to deserve its reputation. Its operating expenditure per pupil in 1961–62 was over $1,000, well above the national average for suburban high schools, and almost double that of non-suburban districts. The faculty of approximately three hundred teachers, most with master's degrees and many with Ph.D.'s, is well paid. The average teaching experience of the faculty members is twelve years, and one-third have over twenty years' experience. The teacher-student ratio is 1:15. The school's buildings and equipment, located on twenty-seven acres in Winnetka, are valued at over $15,000,000.

New Trier's curriculum is 85 per cent academic, including courses in Russian and Chinese (taught in Russian), and the students have demonstrated their ability to cope with it. Approximately 80 per cent of New Trier graduates score above the national median on standardized tests of aptitude and achievement such as the National Merit Scholarship Examination, and New Trier ranks high among high schools in number of students who become Merit finalists and receive commendation letters. Probably the clearest indicator of the school's excellence and the ability of its student body is the percentage of its graduates that go on to some kind of higher education; approximately 90 per cent of New Trier's graduates continue their education, compared with a national average of about 50 per cent.[2]

New Trier's hard-earned level of excellence has been seriously threatened, according to a number of concerned resi-

[1] James B. Conant, *Slums and Suburbs: A Commentary on Schools in Metropolitan Areas* (New York: McGraw-Hill Book Co., 1961), p. 82.
[2] *Ibid.*, p. 81.

dents, by the district's slow response to post–World War II social change in the community. This change, primarily increasing size and social diversity of the population, created the conditions for one of the most serious social altercations experienced in the traditionally peaceful community of New Trier. The conflict culminated in a series of events between 1961 and 1964, but its roots lay in the historical development of the district and its organization as a political system.

## *The First Fifty Years (1899–1950)*

New Trier Township High School District is located on the western shore of Lake Michigan, approximately fifteen miles north of the Chicago Loop. Until 1850 this area, then known as Grosse Pointe, was unincorporated, but in that year its 473 residents decided that some form of local government was desirable. A new state law, adapted from New England, allowed for the incorporation of part of a county into a township, and the area of about thirty-six square miles bounded by the lake (east), Evanston (south), the Cook County line (north), and the Skokie marshes (west) became New Trier Township, named for Trier, Prussia, the city of origin of many of its settlers.

The population of the township remained stable until after the Civil War, when the suburban movement had its start. The first villages to incorporate within the township were Winnetka and Glencoe (1869), followed by Wilmette (1872) and Kenilworth (1896). The village of Grosse Pointe incorporated in 1874, but was annexed by Wilmette in 1926. By 1880 the population of New Trier Township had grown to 1,500, and by 1890 it had increased to 2,800.

The continued rapid growth of the area in the 1890's raised the question of the accommodation of the increasing number of high school students in the township, most of whom were attending Evanston and Chicago schools. To cope with this situation the New Trier villages took advantage of the provisions of the Illinois School Code authorizing the establishment of township high schools, and in 1899 the New Trier Township High School District was established. A five-member Board of Education was elected in May of that year; by gentlemen's agreement each of the five township villages—Winnetka, Glencoe, Wilmette, Grosse Pointe, and Kenilworth—was represented.

The Board's first session was held on May 19, 1899, when it was decided to hold a referendum election on July 29 to determine the site of the new high school. The voters selected a six-acre "wilderness" located in Winnetka just north of the Kenilworth line, where, according to one report, "houses were unknown." A $60,000 referendum on August 5, which would authorize the Board to buy the site and build a school, created considerable controversy but was passed in spite of a large number of dissenting votes. Construction of the school—one large tower building, which survived until 1954—was begun immediately and completed in February, 1901.

Despite the fact that the township had doubled its population between 1890 and 1900 (to 5,400), the initial enrollment was only 76. The small number of prospective students, along with the limited resources of the individual villages, had no doubt been an important factor in the decision to build a township school rather than separate schools in each of the township villages. Kenilworth, with a total population of 300 in 1900, was presumably unable to support a high school of its own, as were Glencoe (1,000), Winnetka (1,800), and Wilmette (2,300). In the next decade, however, the high school enrollment increased fivefold (to 348), while the population of New Trier Township again doubled (to 10,700). In each of the next two decades both the student body and the township doubled, so that by 1930 New Trier High School had an enrollment of 1,801, and the district a population of 35,200.

In these twenty-nine years the school's physical plant had

kept pace with its growing student body, increasing the investment of the New Trier community in a centralized high
school system. In 1907 a manual arts building was added, and
in 1909 a west wing to the tower building was completed;
three years later the school site was expanded to fifteen acres
so that an assembly and dining hall and an east wing to the
tower, housing gymnasiums and study halls, could be
constructed. In 1921 the campus was enlarged to twenty-seven
acres. It was necessary to add a new dining hall in 1923, an
expanded heating plant in 1926, and a larger gymnasium in
1928.

Community identity with the high school was also
strengthened by the local, state-wide, and even national reputation it was building. One obviously biased reviewer, writing
during the quarto-centennial of the school in 1926, spoke of
New Trier as "a model institution after which schools in many
states are patterning their curriculum, their teaching methods,
even their plan of buildings."[3] Soon thereafter (1931)
Matthew Gaffney became superintendent and principal of
New Trier, and until his resignation, for reasons of health, in
1954, he devoted his considerable skills to fulfilling New
Trier's motto—"Not the biggest but the best." In the eyes of
most district residents he succeeded, and in the process developed intensive community loyalty to, and support of, the
township school.

During the Depression decade of the 1930's, township
growth dropped off significantly, to 10 per cent of the 1930
figure. At the same time the New Trier enrollment increased
almost 50 per cent, so that by 1940 it reached 2,653, a peak
not to be surpassed until 1955. But even the Depression did
not stop New Trier's plant expansion. In 1931 the industrial
arts building, and in 1933 the north classroom building were
completed, and even though the 1933 Board of Education
considered closing the high school in the fall of 1935 because

[3] *Wilmette Life*, June 11, 1926, p. 34.

delays in tax collections had resulted in a lack of funds, a natatorium with an Olympic-size pool was nevertheless constructed in 1936.

During the 1940's the township population remained relatively stable, gaining only about 3 per cent, while high school enrollment by 1948 had decreased to its lowest point since 1934 (2,204), before beginning an upward spiral that is not expected to level off until the 1970's. In this decade, the first addition to the campus in fourteen years was begun—the music-speech-drama building, which was completed in 1950.

The social and demographic changes that took place in the community between 1950 and 1963 (during which time the student body increased from 2,260 to 4,800) had significant consequences for the New Trier educational system. During this period five referenda were held (1953, 1957, 1961, 1962, and 1963) in a belated effort to expand the District's facilities to keep pace with its enrollment growth and to maintain its high academic standards. The results were a renovated and enlarged "old" New Trier (1953–57), the addition of an eighteen-acre athletic area (1957–59), and the authorization for the Board to purchase a site and construct a second high school (1961–63), at a total cost to District taxpayers of $16,450,000.[4] This physical expansion was achieved only at the expense of a series of acrimonious social conflicts within the New Trier community, including the first two referendum defeats ever suffered by a New Trier Board of Education. Chapter Two will be concerned with exploring in detail the

---

[4] The five referenda and their outcomes were as follows:

| YEAR | PURPOSE | COST | OUTCOME |
|------|---------|------|---------|
| 1953 | renovation and expansion of plant | $5,875,000 | carried |
| 1957 | seven-acre site increase | 900,000 | failed |
| 1961 | forty-acre site for second school | 975,000 | failed |
| 1962 | forty-acre site for second school | 1,825,000 | carried |
| 1963 | second high school | 8,750,000 | carried |

social and political causes and consequences of educational policy in these conflicts.

### New Trier as a Political System

For most educators, and indeed for many other citizens, to associate education with politics is to commit the most grievous of sins. To these people the fact that the schools have been removed from municipal control and placed in a special uni-functional jurisdiction, administered by highly trained professionals, with nonpartisan election of school boards, removes education from the "dirty" world of politics and all that that word implies.

Thomas H. Eliot, among others, has disputed this argument:

> . . . School districts are governmental units, . . . school board members and school superintendents are engaged in political activity whether they like it or not. Public schools are part of government. They are political entities. They are a fit subject for study by political scientists.[5]

Not only is public education "political," argues another political scientist, but in terms of function, structure, and legal standing, it has all the characteristics of a political system.

> It has a defined geographical jurisdiction, a specified range of purposes, a recognizedly "public" character, a constituency, mechanisms for popular selection and control of decision-makers, a legislative body, an executive, a bureaucracy, and fiscal powers. Like other local political jurisdictions, it is established and run according to laws of the state.[6]

One must be careful not to accept the school district as just another political system. Traditionally, education has occupied a favored position in the hierarchy of public services;

---

[5] Thomas H. Eliot, "Toward an Understanding of Public School Politics," *American Political Science Review*, LIII (December, 1959), 1035.

[6] David W. Minar, "School, Community, and Politics in Suburban Areas," in B. J. Chandler *et al.* (eds.), *Education in Urban Society* (New York: Dodd, Mead, and Co., 1962), p. 91.

a general consensus has developed, based ultimately on Jeffersonian ideology, concerning the value of a good educational system. An individual is against education at the risk of community opprobrium, although conflict is common over sub-issues—personnel, curriculum, school finance, district organization, and facilities—wherever communities are unable to agree on explicit criteria of a "good" educational system.[7]

In the light of the foregoing, it seems appropriate to include in this profile a brief sketch of the formal and informal political organization of the New Trier District. A knowledge of this organization will be of assistance in understanding the course of community conflict and process of integration to be described and analyzed in the next two chapters. The "recognizedly 'public' character" of the school system is assumed, as is its "specified range of purposes."

(a) *The framework of state law:* The formal operation of all school districts in Illinois is governed by the School Code[8] and the administrative policies of the State Superintendent of Public Instruction. Occasional reference to the Code is made in the discussion of the operation of high school districts in this section.

(b) *Defined geographical jurisdiction:* The geographical boundaries of the New Trier Township High School District have been altered very little since its organization in 1899. At that time its jurisdiction was coterminous with that of New Trier Township. Since 1950, the District has been expanded by the addition of three small areas from two adjoining townships, as permitted by Illinois law:

> The boundaries of existing school districts lying entirely within any county may be changed by detachment, annexa-

---

[7] See the discussion of school controversies in James S. Coleman, *Community Conflict* (Glencoe, Ill.: The Free Press, 1957).

[8] *The School Code of Illinois*, Circular Series A, No. 146 (Springfield: Office of the Superintendent of Public Instruction, 1961).

tion, division, dissolution or consolidation or any combination thereof by the county board of trustees of such county when petitioned by the boards of each district affected or by a majority of the legal voters residing in each district affected or by two-thirds of the legal voters residing in any territory proposed to be detached from one or more districts or in each of one or more districts proposed to be annexed to or consolidated with another district.[9]

In 1955, a minute area of Niles Township, which abuts the Glenview section to the south, was included within New Trier's jurisdiction. A significantly larger area had been added when the residents of Northfield and several small segments of Northbrook Village west of the District voted to be included in 1952. At the time, Northfield Township did not have a high school of its own and sent its students to New Trier High School on a tuition basis. A school was being contemplated for the Northfield area in the near future, but Northfield parents with close familial and social ties to Winnetka chose to incur the larger tax burden in order to maintain them, and of course to insure that their children could attend a school of proven excellence. The inclusion of Northfield in the District became an event of considerable consequence in 1961, when the Board of Education chose to locate the second high school there.

Within the geographical jurisdiction of New Trier High School District are included a number of political jurisdictions. In addition to Northfield and parts of Glenview, Northbrook, and Skokie, the New Trier District is composed of four of the wealthiest suburban municipalities in the United States—Glencoe, Winnetka, Kenilworth, and Wilmette. A second set of governments within the District is made up of its six elementary school systems—Glencoe, Winnetka, Kenilworth, Wilmette, Avoca, and Sunset Ridge. Third are the various park districts throughout the community. A fourth

[9] *Ibid.*, Sec. 7–1.

political unit, a part of which wends its way through all of these, and which played an important role in the controversy of 1961–63, is the Cook County Forest Preserve District, administered by the Cook County Board of Commissioners.

(c) *Constituency:* In 1960 the New Trier High School District had a constituency of approximately 65,000, of whom approximately 39,000 were eligible to vote in District elections and referenda.[10] As has been generally true throughout the nation, New Trier voters have been traditionally apathetic toward the governance of their District. School Board trustees were elected (candidacies were never contested) and referenda were invariably approved by a small percentage of the potential electorate, until the rapid growth of the District following World War II necessitated large and expensive expansion of facilities. Since the expansion referendum of 1953, when a voter turn-out record was set, the interest of the electorate in school policies has so increased that 50 per cent of those eligible voted in the 1962 referendum. The development of interest in policy has not been matched with increased interest in candidates for the Board; elections are still uncontested, and voter turnout is about 2 per cent.

(d) *Legislature:* In Illinois, the legislative branch of the school district is the board of education, consisting of seven members elected at large with overlapping three-year terms. In New Trier, members are limited by common consent to two terms, in order to give "a number of citizens an opportunity for this public service," and virtually all members serve for six years.[11] Candidates in New Trier have been slated by a District caucus since 1955, but in other districts they may be

---

[10] The Illinois School Code provides that, to be eligible to vote in a school election, one must be a United States citizen, twenty-one years old or older; he must have been a resident of the state for one year, of the county for ninety days, and of the school district for thirty days immediately preceding the election (School Code, Sec. 9–3).

[11] *Rules for the New Trier High School Board Caucus* (as amended to March 1, 1962), p. 8.

nominated by retiring board members, political parties, or interest groups, or on a self-selection basis. Although the members are theoretically elected at large from the District, geographical representation has been in effect in New Trier since the first board election in 1899. At first, each of the five villages—Glencoe, Winnetka, Kenilworth, Wilmette, and Grosse Pointe—was represented by one member. When Grosse Pointe was annexed by Wilmette in 1926, Wilmette was assigned two representatives. Since that time, Illinois high school boards have been increased to seven members by state law, and the distribution, based more or less on population, is as follows: Glencoe, 2; Wilmette, 2; Winnetka, 2; and Northfield, 1.

(e) *Executive:* The Illinois School Code provides that one of the members of the board be elected president by his fellow members for a term of one year. The only statutory duties he has are to "preside at all meetings, and . . . perform such duties as are imposed upon him by law or by action of the Board of Education."[12] In most districts, however, the *de facto* executive is the superintendent appointed by the board to administer the district. The superintendent plays much the same role as the city manager in municipal government, where expertise has enhanced their political leadership function at the expense of the elected officials.[13]

(f) *Bureaucracy:* The significance of the bureaucracy in the organization of a school district depends on the bureaucracy's size and the number and type of policy decisions the board is called on to make. School Board members, who have ultimate responsibility for selecting the bureaucracy, are in

[12] School Code, Secs. 10–13.
[13] See Robert C. Wood's discussion of this phenomenon in *Suburbia: Its People and Politics* (Boston: Houghton Mifflin Co., 1959); also James B. Holderman, *Decision-Making and Community Leadership in the Village of Winnetka, Illinois* (unpublished Ph.D. dissertation, Northwestern University, 1962).

many cases busy citizens who can afford to spend little more time on school business than is required by the monthly board meeting. The day-to-day administration of the district is performed by the superintendent, his staff, and the faculty; but often, by virtue of their educational expertise, they make or strongly influence major policy decisions that are the responsibility of the board. In New Trier, there is every indication that Superintendent Matthew Gaffney played a major role in shaping District policy from 1931 to his retirement in 1954. While his successor's style differs from that of Gaffney, there is no reason to believe that William Cornog has been any less influential in shaping policy during the District's most dynamic growth period.

At least three other groups may operate within the bureaucratic framework of a school system. To differentiate them from administrative staff and faculty, Alger's concept of the "external bureaucracy" is useful.[14] The external bureaucracy is comprised of those members of the community who are drawn into the decision-making process while acting as private citizens. In school politics, associations of parents, community organizations, and *ad hoc* study committees fall into this category, and play important quasi-official roles in the policy-making process. In New Trier, the members of the Parents' Association, the League of Women Voters, and the board-appointed *ad hoc* Citizens' Advisory Committee (1961–62) served as external bureaucrats at one time or another during the period of controversy.

(g) *Fiscal powers:* School districts, like other local governmental units in Illinois, are empowered to levy taxes to provide the revenue necessary to carry out their functions. In most communities, but particularly in the suburban areas—where rapid growth requires constant expansion—school taxes constitute a significant portion of the tax dollar. The latest

---

[14] Chadwick F. Alger, "The External Bureaucracy in United States Foreign Affairs," *Administrative Science Quarterly*, VII (June, 1962), 50–78.

available national data (1955–56) show that an average of 42 per cent of suburban school district revenue comes from local taxes, emphasizing the high value placed on local control of education. In Illinois as a whole the figure is 51.9 per cent; in New Trier it is 84.3 per cent.[15]

Maintaining local control of educational financing in the fast-growing suburban districts requires frequent tax-rate increases, and bond referenda, to keep pace with the communities' demands for curriculum excellence and uncrowded classrooms. These demands often result in heated social conflicts when they are not matched by a willingness to pay higher taxes. Suburban districts throughout the nation are suffering referenda defeats as they are caught up in so-called "taxpayer revolts."

Illinois law provides that high school boards "may levy a tax annually, at not to exceed the maximum rates and for the specified purposes, upon all the taxable property of the district," as follows: (a) for building purposes, .1875 per cent; (b) for educational purposes, .65 per cent; and (c) for transportation, when applicable, .02 per cent. Within these limits, boards may increase rates as they deem necessary, but most suburban districts have found it necessary to exceed one or more of them. The School Code allows for such increases—to .25 per cent for building, 1.60 per cent for education, and .10 per cent for transportation—but requires that a referendum be held to secure public approval.[16]

The Code also authorizes high school boards to borrow money for "the purpose of building, equipping, altering, or repairing school buildings, or purchasing or improving school

---

[15] Office of Education, U.S. Department of Health, Education and Welfare, *Statistics of Local School Systems: 1955–56* (Washington, D.C.: U.S. Government Printing Office, 1960), p. 31. Nationally, the other sources of revenue are: state, 20.9 per cent; non-revenue receipts, 19.2 per cent; other, 8.2 per cent; local appropriations, 5.2 per cent; county, 2.8 per cent; and federal, 1.7 per cent.

[16] School Code, Secs. 17–3, 17–4, 17–5.

sites, or acquiring and equipping . . . recreation grounds, . . . or for the purpose of purchasing a site . . ."[17] by issuing twenty-year bonds, but stipulates that a proposition authorizing the board to issue them must be approved by a majority of the votes cast in a referendum. The Illinois constitution restricts the amount of bonded indebtedness of any district to 5 per cent of the district's assessed valuation.[18]

(h) *Popular selection and control of decision-makers:* Like other political systems, school districts provide mechanisms for selecting decision-makers and for exercising control over the decisions that they make. As indicated above, Illinois school boards are elected for three-year terms by each district's eligible voters. In most cases these terms overlap, an arrangement which necessitates an election each year and makes it difficult for any one bloc to wrest control of the board in a single election. The degree to which these offices are contested varies from district to district and depends in large part on the method of candidate nomination. In districts where party or self-nomination is found, the likelihood of contested elections is higher than in those districts where retiring board members select their successors, or, as in New Trier, where a caucus of representative individuals endorses a slate of candidates.

The use of the caucus system does not necessarily obviate a contested election, especially during the transition to that system, but the probability is reduced. The caucus, a form of one-party nonpartisanship which fits the image of apolitical school politics, varies as to the source of its "representativeness." In some districts the caucus accepts delegates from any community-wide organization—civic, religious, or social—and a large and unwieldy group is often the result. A second type consists of a self-appointed elite group with some community stature who meet to select nominees. Third, there

[17] *Ibid.*, Sec. 19–3.
[18] Illinois Constitution, Article IX.

are caucuses that are geographically representative. New Trier is of this last type.

Until 1955, the New Trier Board of Education was a self-perpetuating body. Its members served one or two terms and then had the responsibility of selecting successors from their respective villages and circulating petitions on their behalf. Exceptions were Glencoe, where candidates were selected by the elementary school district caucus, and Kenilworth, where they were selected by a Citizens' Advisory Committee. Through the efforts of village branches of the League of Women Voters, the New Trier Township Citizens' League, the caucuses of the various elementary school districts, and the members of the Board of Education, a New Trier High School District Caucus was organized in 1954 and nominated its first candidates the following year. The Caucus, whose stated purpose is "to select on a nonpartisan basis and present candidates" for the High School Board of Education, is composed of delegates from each of the district's elementary school districts, selected by "the local body which has the responsibility of nominating candidates for members of the elementary school board."[19] The apportionment of delegates among the elementary districts is based on an unspecified combination of population and assessed valuation which preserves power in the older districts at the expense of the newer and faster-growing areas. Rapid population increases in the District have resulted in two changes in the composition of the Caucus within the last three years; from twenty delegates in 1961, it was enlarged to twenty-five in 1962, and to thirty in 1963, to give more representation to the growing areas without reducing the number of delegates from the relatively static districts.

Ordinarily, three meetings of the Caucus are held each

[19] *Rules for the New Trier High School Board Caucus* (as amended to March 1, 1962), p. 2.

year. The first, taking place at least forty-five days prior to the petition-filing date for Board candidates, is an organizational meeting at which data sheets on proposed candidates are distributed to Caucus delegates. At the second meeting, held within three weeks after the first, the qualifications of all proposed candidates are discussed, including those of incumbents who desire renomination. At this meeting incumbents can be renominated by a two-thirds vote of the delegates. The last Caucus meeting, two weeks after the second, involves a secret ballot to select the rest of the candidates by majority vote from among the nominees.

Candidates for election to the School Board have never been challenged in New Trier, although in recent years there has been some talk of write-in campaigns, and some reports that Caucus delegates have not been in complete accord over the candidates ultimately selected. Some of this comment is personal (i.e., the individual criticizing a certain nomination feels the candidate is not fully qualified for the position); part of it is based on inter-village jealousy concerning representation on the Board; and still more of it represents a protest against School Board policy.

Although the citizens of New Trier have very little direct choice in the selection of school policy makers,[20] Illinois law provides them with opportunities to check policy involving major expenditures. All tax-rate increases over and above the limits discussed in section (g) above require voter approval. New Trier held a rate referendum in 1958, when an increase in the education levy easily gained approval. Also requiring voter approval are all Board decisions to borrow money to implement policies. Since World War II five bond referenda have been held (1953, 1957, 1961, 1962, 1963). As previously noted, the results of these included the first two

[20] They are in fact at least twice removed from the selection process. High School Caucus delegates are selected by the elementary district caucuses, only one of which (Glencoe) has elected members. (See below, pp. 27–33.)

defeats ever suffered by a New Trier Board (1957, 1961), imbuing it with a new respect for the wishes of the district electorate.

## Political and Social Characteristics of the Plural Community

Having traced the historical development of the New Trier High School District and described the formal and informal structure of the District as a political system, it remains to profile the social and political characteristics of the municipalities that make up the plural community. Such an exercise will facilitate the description of the case study in social conflict to be presented in the following chapter and the analysis of the case in terms of political integration in Chapter Three.

### Social Structure

The social structure of the New Trier plural community can best be understood in terms of the social characteristics of the five villages that compose that community—Glencoe, Winnetka, Kenilworth, Wilmette, and Northfield.

These are all old (with the exception of Northfield, all were incorporated between 1869 and 1896), established, affluent "bedroom" suburbs, populated in the main by upper-middle-class and upper-class professional people and corporation executives who commute to the Chicago Loop. Compared with the entire suburban area of metropolitan Chicago, the residents of the New Trier villages in general are wealthier, older, and more highly educated, and the populations grow less rapidly (see Table 1). The District's population (64,300 in 1960) is primarily white, Anglo-Saxon, and Protestant, although there are small Negro enclaves (remnants of service families) in Winnetka and Glencoe, large Jewish

## TABLE 1

Social, Economic, and Demographic Characteristics
of All Metropolitan Chicago Suburbs Compared
with Those of New Trier Municipalities, 1960[a]

| Characteristic | All Chi. Suburbs | Glencoe | Win-netka | Kenil-worth | Wil-mette | North-field |
|---|---|---|---|---|---|---|
| **Demographic:** | | | | | | |
| Pop., 1960 | 2,670,509 | 10,472 | 13,368 | 2,959 | 28,268 | 4,005 |
| Pop., 1950 | 1,556,906 | 6,980 | 12,105 | 2,789 | 18,162 | 1,426 |
| % growth, 1950–60 | 71.5 | 50.0 | 10.4 | 6.1 | 55.6 | 180.9 |
| % pop. under 5 | 12.4 | 8.0 | 7.0 | 7.0 | 11.0 | 13.0 |
| % pop. under 18 | 37.4 | 38.0 | 34.0 | 35.0 | 38.0 | 41.0 |
| % pop. 65 and over | 7.0 | 6.0 | 10.0 | 9.0 | 9.0 | 4.0 |
| % pop. non-white | 3.1 | 6.5 | 2.0 | 1.3 | 0.8 | 0.7 |
| Med. age, 1960 | 29.2 | 35.0 | 38.0 | 39.0 | 32.0 | 31.0 |
| **Socio-economic:** | | | | | | |
| Med. school yrs. cmptd. | 12.1 | 14.4 | 15.2 | 15.3 | 13.8 | 13.9 |
| Med. fam. incm. | $8,158 | $20,136 | $20,166 | $20,000[b] | $13,661 | $15,000[b] |
| % fam. w/ incm. $10,000 & over | 32.1 | 77.3 | 79.2 | 83.9 | 68.4 | 65.4 |
| % prof'l—mgr'l | 25.3 | 49.1 | 52.6 | 60.8 | 47.1 | 48.5 |
| % craftsmn-oprtvs | 32.2 | 4.7 | 4.8 | 2.9 | 8.8 | 13.7 |
| **Housing:** | | | | | | |
| % units in struct. blt. before 1940 | 43.3 | 57.0 | 77.0 | 72.0 | 54.0 | 18.0 |
| % units in struct. blt. after 1950 | 43.6 | 36.0 | 16.0 | 14.0 | 38.0 | 64.0 |
| % units owner occ'd | 76.2 | 89.0 | 84.2 | 93.9 | 86.6 | 89.9 |
| Med. value of homes | $18,900 | $35,000+ | $35,000+ | $35,000+ | $33,000 | $33,000 |

[a] Source: Adapted from Northeastern Illinois Metropolitan Area Planning Commission, *Suburban Fact-book* (Chicago, 1962). The NIMAPC data were adapted from various 1960 Bureau of the Census reports.
[b] Estimated. Specific amounts for municipalities of under 10,000 population not given in Bureau of the Census reports.

groups in Glencoe and west Wilmette, and a considerable Catholic population in west Wilmette.

In terms of our interest in the social and political integration of these villages *vis à vis* the policy-making process of the larger system of which they are a part, the differences in social structure *among* the villages rather than the differences *between* the New Trier community and the suburban area as a whole are of primary significance. It is in these differences that one may logically expect to find some clues to the origin of social conflict in the community.

Table 1, based on 1960 data, reveals a great deal about the socio-economic-demographic similarities and differences among the New Trier villages. There is apparently a considerable degree of homogeneity among them, as evidenced by the position they share relative to the median figures for all the Chicago suburbs. This is corroborated by the Composite Socio-Economic-Status Rank assigned to each suburban community by the Northeast Illinois Metropolitan Area Planning Commission. Using a fifteen-position scale (1 to 15 from high to low), each Chicago suburb was ranked on the basis of four indicators: (a) median number of school years completed, (b) median family income, (c) percentage of families with an income of $10,000 or more, and (d) percentage of employed persons with white-collar occupations. Each of the five municipalities in the New Trier District was assigned a "1."[21]

Nevertheless, there are significant differences among the five villages. They vary considerably in population size; two are under 5,000 (Kenilworth and Northfield), two are in the 10,000–15,000 category (Glencoe and Winnetka), and one is almost 30,000 (Wilmette). More importantly, the villages vary in their rate of growth; both Winnetka and Kenilworth, with very little undeveloped land, grew slowly during the 1950–60 decade (with increases of 10.4 per cent and 6.1 per cent respectively), while Glencoe (50 per cent) and Wilmette (55.6 per cent) increased by half. Northfield, the newest and least developed village, experienced the most rapid

[21] Northeastern Illinois Metropolitan Area Planning Commission, *Suburban Factbook* (Chicago, 1962), Table 8.

growth by far (180.9 per cent), and shows indications of continuing this trend.

Northfield presents an interesting contrast to the other New Trier communities. Founded fifty-seven years after the oldest municipality in the District and thirty years after the next youngest, and not established as a full-fledged member of the New Trier District until 1952, it manifests its newness in a number of ways. Its population is younger than those of its neighbors; 41 per cent are under eighteen years of age, 13 per cent under five, and only 4 per cent over sixty-five, with a median age of thirty-one. This characteristic, particularly the proportion of the population under eighteen, has important implications for the relative investment of the community in the educational system. Its housing structures are significantly newer than those of the other communities; only 18 per cent of those existing in 1960 had been built by 1940, and 64 per cent were constructed after 1950. Somewhat fewer of its relatively youthful breadwinners are earning $10,000 or more (65.4 per cent), and more of them are employed as craftsmen-operatives (13.7 per cent) than in the other four villages.

But in other respects, e.g., educational level, owner occupation of homes, median value of homes, percentage of labor force in professional-managerial positions, and median family income, Northfield ranks equal to, or higher than, at least one other village, in most cases Wilmette. In addition, the residents of Northfield have close familial and social ties with Winnetkans which draw them into the New Trier community; many of them are former Winnetkans (or the progeny of Winnetkans) who, unable to find available lots in Winnetka, had homes built in adjacent Northfield. The close relationship is symbolized by the joint sponsorship of organizations, activities, and services by the two villages—the League of Women Voters, churches, service organizations, the park district, the library, the health department, and the post office. Even the Northfield village fathers are former Winnetkans. In fact, the

Winnetka-Northfield ties are close enough that there is talk of annexation of Northfield by Winnetka as soon as the former raises the level of its village services to a par with those of Winnetka, so that Winnetkans will not have to pay extra taxes to develop the newer area.

If one were to arrange the five villages on a continuum based on the four indicators used by the NIMAPC (educational level, family income, incomes of $10,000 and more, and white-collar occupations), they would rank as follows: Kenilworth, Winnetka, Glencoe, and Wilmette and Northfield about even. This ranking was generally reinforced by residents of the District during interviews for this study, although most felt that Kenilworth's small size forced it to abdicate any claim it might otherwise make to leadership in the District. Respondents indicated that Winnetka had traditionally held this position, particularly in the development of quality education. For example, a group of Winnetkans strongly urged in the 1920's that the New Trier community should strive to build a high school system of such excellence that there would be no need to send a child to private school to give him a good education. This same group led the campaign which resulted in the attainment of that goal.

As indicated above, the population of the District is not readily differentiated on an ethnic basis. In each of the five villages, a large majority of residents are no less than second-generation native American Caucasians, and many of those who are of "foreign stock"[22] trace their origin to three countries—the United Kingdom, Canada, and Germany (see Table 2).

Religious affiliation, although exceedingly difficult to ascertain because it is not systematically recorded by any

[22] The Bureau of the Census defines "foreign stock" as "the foreign-born population combined with the native population of foreign or mixed parentage." *United States Census of Population and Housing: 1960 Census Tracts* (Final Report, PHC [1]-26; Washington, D.C.: U.S. Government Printing Office, 1962), p. 3.

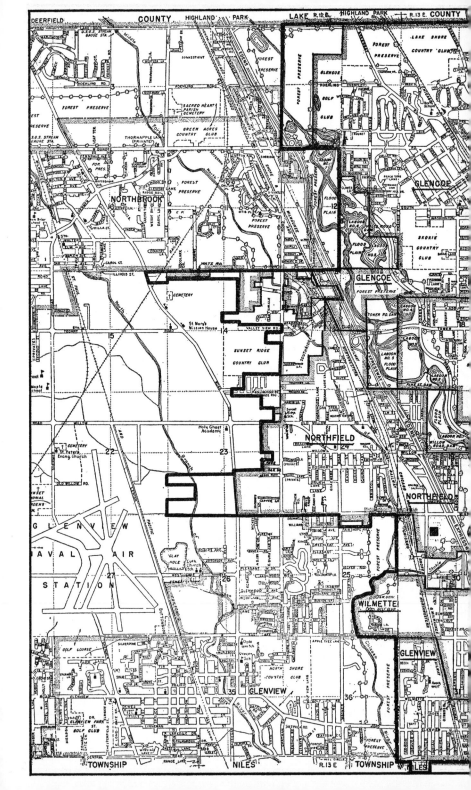

FIGURE 1. NEW TRIER TOWNSHIP HIGH SCHOOL DISTRICT

■ New Trier Township High School West

● New Trier Township High School East

## TABLE 2

Foreign Stock as a Percentage of Total Population, and
Per Cent of Foreign Stock from United Kingdom,
Canada, and Germany, by New Trier Villages

|  | F.S. as %<br>Total Pop. | % F.S. from<br>United Kingdom | % F.S. from<br>Canada | % F.S. from<br>Germany |
|---|---|---|---|---|
| Glencoe | 35.0ᵃ | 6.8 | 6.2 | 11.3 |
| Winnetka | 22.7 | 8.7 | 13.0 | 19.1 |
| Kenilworth | 19.5 | 19.7 | 24.6 | 13.9 |
| Wilmette | 26.4 | 10.7 | 7.8 | 17.3 |
| Northfield | 27.5(est.) | 6.8(est.) | 8.6(est.) | 17.3(est.) |

ᵃ Of Glencoe's foreign stock, 36.9 per cent originated in the U.S.S.R.—an indication, according to one interpretation of census data, of a Jewish population; see Leonard Broom and Eshref Shevky, "The Differentiation of an Ethnic Group," *American Sociological Review* (August, 1949).

public or private agency, is one means of distinguishing among several of the villages in the New Trier community. In two municipalities there are large concentrations of Jews. The Anti-Defamation League of B'nai B'rith in Chicago, while admitting that it has no accurate data on the Jewish population of suburban communities, estimates that approximately half of Glencoe and approximately 20 per cent of Wilmette are Jewish.[23] There are a few Jewish families in Winnetka, fewer still in Northfield, and none in Kenilworth (see Table 3).

The Anti-Defamation League stresses that there is a vast cultural difference, of which both groups are cognizant, between the major concentrations of Jews in New Trier. The Glencoe group consists largely of pre-1890 German immigrants and their descendants; they first settled in the Hyde Park section of south Chicago, and then moved directly to Glencoe in the early decades of the twentieth century. They are quite wealthy, live in $40,000–$150,000 homes, and are considered "natives" of the community. The Wilmette group,

[23] Interview with Albert Weiss, Research Director, Chicago Anti-Defamation League of B'nai B'rith, March 6, 1963.

## TABLE 3

### Jews as a Pecentage of Total New Residents in New Trier Municipalities, 1956–59[a]

| Village | 1956 | 1957 | 1958 | 1959 | Total 1956–59 |
|---|---|---|---|---|---|
| Glencoe | 54.2 | 49.3 | 41.7 | 49.6 | 48.7 |
| Winnetka | 10.0 | 10.1 | 6.2 | 6.8 | 8.2 |
| Kenilworth[b] | 0.0 | 0.0 | 0.0 | 0.0 | 0.0 |
| Wilmette | 22.8 | 28.5 | 26.9 | 28.4 | 27.6 |
| Northfield | 2.7 | 2.4 | 2.3 | 7.3 | 3.8 |

[a] Source: Data compiled by the Anti-Defamation League of B'nai B'rith, Chicago, Illinois, based on "religious preference" item of village "Welcomer" lists. The League abandoned the project after this four-year period.

[b] According to the Chicago Anti-Defamation League, there are only one or two Jewish families in Kenilworth, and these are long-time residents with considerable wealth.

on the other hand, is comprised primarily of 1890–1920 immigrants (and their descendants) from Russia, Poland, and other Eastern European countries who settled first on the west side of Chicago (Lawndale). They are less wealthy, and they arrived in suburbia only after a series of moves within the city—North Kedzie, East Rogers Park, and West Rogers Park. Those that have settled in Wilmette are concentrated in an area of newly built, moderately priced tract houses (the only ones in the New Trier District) in the southwestern section of Wilmette. They are considered "newcomers" and "outsiders" and seldom or never interact with the "native" Jews of Glencoe. Most of these people made considerable sacrifices and put themselves deeply in debt in order to live in Wilmette and send their children to New Trier High School. Consequently they have a keen interest in school policy.

There are a fair number of Roman Catholics in the District, judging from the distribution of churches and the percentage of children enrolled in non-public schools. In only one section of the District, however, is there a sizable concentration of Catholics—south-central Wilmette, where a large group of Italian-Americans live. Many of the Catholics in the District are older Rhine Valley Germans, while most of the newer families moving into eastern Wilmette are Irish. It has been estimated that approximately one-half of the population of east Wilmette is Catholic. The fact that these families felt the "double burden" of supporting two Catholic high schools and numerous grade schools in the area, in addition to the public schools, had important implications for the New Trier Board's expansion policies, although a large number of Catholic school eighth-grade graduates transfer to New Trier.

In summary, it might be said that the population of the New Trier District is more homogeneous than not in terms of occupation, educational level, and income—i.e., that "life-styles" are generally similar. On the other hand, there are some variations in religious affiliations and length of residence in the community which have important consequences for the way the District behaves in reaction to proposed School Board policy.

### Political Structure

One of the more persistent myths concerning the American educational system is that the public function performed is somehow unique and therefore requires unique institutional arrangements and a special decision-making process. It is argued that school government ought to be non-partisan and indeed even non-political. Some observers have pointed out that municipal and school government in suburbia can be distinguished by the extreme apolitical façade of the latter, which results in a difference in public orientation and subsequently in behavior.[24]

This does not seem to be the case in New Trier Township. The political structures of the five township villages are very similar to the political structure of the New Trier High School District. In both cases, the public demands the best

---

[24] Minar, "School, Community, and Politics," pp. 90–104; also Wood, *Suburbia*, p. 189.

possible service with the least possible effort and is willing to pay administrative experts top salaries to achieve this. All five municipalities are "dormitory" suburbs for the city of Chicago; their male populations have a considerable amount of their attention diverted from the activity of suburbia in favor of professional and managerial concerns downtown. The time they spend in the suburbs they expect to spend enjoying the amenities of life without concerning themselves with village politics. To this end, each of these villages has organized itself so as to avoid social conflict and achieve administrative efficiency. Because each community is relatively homogeneous in social make-up, without the stratification which would yield a natural elite, each has resorted to government by "technical authority"—that is, by professional administrators who know how to provide public services efficiently and without controversy. Superficially, the municipalities are governed by elected boards of trustees, but in practice these part-time honorific officials relinquish the day-to-day administration and a great many of the major policy decisions to their professional village managers. The highly-educated residents of these communities have great respect for expertise and put great stock in the managers' solutions to local problems. In many respects the superintendent of New Trier High School serves a similar function in the school system.

There are other analogies between the political structure of New Trier's villages and that of its High School District. For example, the caucus method of nomination and election is used for both school and village officials, although there are some variations among villages in procedure.

The caucus system of candidate selection is essentially a one-party, nonpartisan system. Groups of citizens representing civic and social organizations or geographical areas in the community meet prior to elections to interview possible candidates for elective office and to select the most qualified. In most communities employing this system, those in New Trier among them, nomination by the caucus is tantamount to election, in the absence of other party organizations, since write-in campaigns are seldom effective. The motto of the caucus system states that "the office seeks the man and never the man the office." Its advocates argue that such a system allows the community to recruit the most capable and qualified citizens on a nonpartisan basis, and, further, that a truly representative caucus will operate to inhibit community conflict in the form of contested elections.

The first village in New Trier to adopt both the village-manager form of government and the caucus system was Winnetka, which did so in 1915 and 1917, respectively. The caucus in Winnetka is an organized political party, officially known as the Caucus Party. Candidates are nominated by a Caucus Committee, whose membership is changed annually but always includes three representatives from each voting precinct and five from the village at large. During the year the committee thoroughly investigates the fitness of possible candidates with regard to the requisites of the public offices to be filled. At the same time, it prepares a platform, which includes suggestions offered by civic organizations and individual citizens. In January of each year, a public Village Caucus Meeting is held at which the committee reviews its activities of the past year; presents its recommended platform containing definite positions with regard to Winnetka government, schools, public utilities, transportation, recreation, and other issues; offers a slate of candidates for village offices; and suggests representatives to the Caucus Committee for the coming year. The general public is then given the opportunity to amend, reject, or approve any or all of the committee's recommendations. These recommendations are almost always approved.

New Trier's smallest village adopted the village-manager system in 1920. Kenilworth has always been nonpartisan, but until 1939 the responsibility for candidate selection and issue articulation fell upon a small and loosely organized group of citizens who met occasionally to discuss community problems. In that year, the Citizens' Advisory Committee was formally established, with a membership composed of the presidents and immediate past presidents of all social and civic organizations in the village. The committee has three stated purposes: (a) "to co-ordinate civic effort," (b) "to act as a nonpartisan committee to suggest candidates for the village, school and park boards," and (c) "to make effective the co-operation of all boards and organizations engaged in civic development."[25] In addition, the committee selects delegates to the New Trier High School District Caucus.

Wilmette, the District's largest village, was the third to switch to village-manager government, as it did in 1930. From 1936 to 1938, Wilmette reverted to the mayor-council system, but a 1939 referendum calling for the return of the manager plan was approved, and this system has been in effect ever since.

Wilmette's political structure is a third variation of the caucus theme. Since 1932, Wilmette has operated in accordance with what is called the "Harmony Plan." The plan functions in the following manner: a Creative Committee, comprised of approximately thirty citizens representing various village civic and social organizations, chooses four delegates and an alternate from each of the village voting precincts; these delegates, when assembled, form the Harmony Convention, whose job it is to screen potential candidates for elective village offices, select a single slate of candidates, and circulate petitions on their behalf. In accordance with the state election laws, the convention's petitions and ballots must carry a party label, but this label is changed at each convention to preserve the "non-party" character of the convention.

Wilmette is larger and its population more heteroge-

[25] *Kenilworth: The First Fifty Years* (Kenilworth, Ill., 1947).

neous than is true of the other villages in the District, and perhaps it was inevitable that there would occasionally be challengers to the Harmony slate. This occurred for the first time in 1949, when the Citizens of Wilmette Party elected two of its candidates to office after an intense campaign and a recount suit which resulted in the unseating of five other Citizen Party candidates. The party put up another slate in 1951, but it was unsuccessful. The 1963 Harmony slate was uncontested, although it is rumored that there is a growing split between the long-time and generally more affluent residents of the Lake Michigan side of Wilmette, and the newer arrivals on the west side of town. The avoidance of overt social conflict is a goal of the Harmony Plan, the stated objectives of which are "to nominate for village offices citizens of unquestionable ability without regard to political affiliation, and to eliminate secret caucus nominations, local political factions, and spoils politics."[26]

It should be noted that the Harmony Convention, unlike the Winnetka Caucus Party and the Kenilworth Citizens' Advisory Committee, does *not* slate candidates for the village school district. This is the function of a separate elementary school district caucus made up of delegates from more than twenty civic organizations. To qualify as a participant, an organization must show that it is non-political and non-religious, that it is not a school employees' group, and that it is village-wide in scope; these qualifications are then passed upon by a credentials committee composed of holdover members of the previous caucus. The function of the school caucus is twofold: (a) to select candidates for the elementary district board of education, and (b) to choose delegates to the New Trier High School District Caucus.

Glencoe, also organized as a council-manager government, offers still another form of caucus-party system.

[26] Mrs. Eugene Weinberg, *Spotlight on Wilmette* (Wilmette League of Women Voters, 1955), p. 66.

Through the 1920's, control of the local governing bodies of this village was in the hands of a small, self-perpetuating elite group, whose position was not contested. In the early 1930's, some of the newer members of the community became dissatisfied with this process and ran candidates of their own. The result was a series of bitterly fought campaigns, which split the community apart for several years. Early in 1936, representatives of both factions met and agreed on a committee of ten to select a slate of candidates to be presented to the town meeting. This committee decided to formalize the process of selecting candidates and submitted the Caucus Plan to the town meeting along with a slate of candidates; both were approved.

The Glencoe plan, like the others, is designed to permit all eligible voters in the community to participate in the nonpartisan selection of "well-qualified, experienced, and respected citizens as candidates for the elective offices of the village."[27] The plan, again like those of the neighboring villages, is predicated on a number of assumptions that reveal a great deal about the political structure of the community:

( a ) The interest of the community is best served by selecting the best available men and women for public office, regardless of party identification.
( b ) It is desirable to give all residents an equal opportunity to take part in the selections, i.e., by suggesting well-qualified residents and policy goals to the Caucus, and voting on them in a town meeting.
( c ) This system avoids "needless" contests.
( d ) Public officials, who give their time and effort to the village without compensation, should be protected against undue pressure from any source and from election contests which are "distasteful to candidates and residents alike."

[27] *The Caucus Plan for Selecting Candidates for Elective Office* (as amended to January 30, 1956); Glencoe, Ill., 1956), p. 3.

(e) The community should be governed by its own citizens in a harmonious, non-political manner.

The mechanics of the plan provides for a nonpartisan nominating committee which meets in caucus to consider nominees; selects a slate of candidates, giving due consideration to candidates' ability, integrity, experience, and geographical location; and presents its choices to the town meeting for ratification. This committee is composed of three members (no more than two of one sex) from each voting precinct, one of whom is a holdover member from the previous committee. A second member is elected by precinct residents, and the third is selected by mutual agreement of the holdover and elected members. There is enough dissatisfaction with this method of representation so that an amendment providing for election of all three precinct representatives is being given serious consideration. In addition to the nominating committee, there is a five-man advisory council elected at the town meeting, whose function it is to organize the town meeting, provide the necessary funds for the operation of the Caucus Plan, maintain the required records, and assure the proper function of the plan by advising the nominating committee whenever necessary. Members of the council shall be "substantial citizens who have rendered the Village some valuable service and have interested themselves in the affairs of the community."[28]

The Glencoe village caucus participates in the selection of elementary school board candidates by appointing five holdover members of the general nominating committee to serve on the fifteen-man school board nominating committee. This latter committee, in addition to slating candidates to the Glencoe board of education, appoints delegates to the New Trier High School District Caucus.

One well-respected resident of Glencoe active in caucus affairs, in describing its political process, extolled these

[28] *Ibid.*, p. 5.

"virtues" of the caucus system: (a) all citizens can participate in the selection of candidates because all are invited and urged to suggest worthy nominees to their precinct representatives; (b) the caucus representatives, unlike political party delegates, use their own judgment in selecting candidates because they are not beholden to anyone; and (c) the village is able to get outstanding people elected to public office who would never run for office under a partisan system because they do not want to get involved in conflicts. But despite these "advantages," a number of recent arrivals in the community are opposed to the caucus system as unrepresentative of their interests.

Northfield has only recently adopted the political structure of its neighbors. Before 1940, Northfield was a German farm community of fewer than 800 people. The village was run by a mayor and council, with the election of both being informally agreed upon by the community leaders. After the war, however, the nature of the village changed considerably. The farm land was converted into housing developments; and the population doubled by 1950 and sextupled by 1960, as suburban commuters replaced rural farmers as the predominant group of residents. By 1956, the village had become large and complex enough to consider changing its political structure. Accordingly, the board of trustees passed a resolution in 1956 establishing a village-administrator system, and it appointed a former Winnetkan to the post. At the same time, the new community leaders decided that the interests of the village would best be served by establishing a formal, but nonpartisan, system of candidate selection. The result was the Northfield Caucus, modeled after the Winnetka plan.

## Summary

The variance in the way politics is structured in the five New Trier communities is small. Nonpartisanship and conflict avoidance are the common themes; technical authority (represented by professional administrators) and the caucus system are the common mechanisms. These villages represent the epitome of "gracious suburban living" in the Chicago metropolitan area and rank among the most highly esteemed suburbs in the nation. Here is where those who have "arrived" reside, and because their community is at the top of the suburban hierarchy, they have a strong interest in maintaining its standards. A high level of public service is demanded, for which the residents are willing to pay. They are less willing to be bothered with administering it; professional public administrators are available for that purpose. Village politics for them is a civic duty without social rewards. Controversy over public policy and partisan competition for public office are seen as a threat to the "good life" and are resented as a disruption. The caucus system of candidate nomination and policy articulation results from the communities' endeavor to avoid social conflict in the process of government. In addition, one of the major functions of the professional administrator in these communities is to contain or suppress social conflict; his job may depend on his ability to do this.[29]

The social and political structures of the five villages of the New Trier plural community affect the way in which the larger political system has attempted to cope with the social and demographic changes which occurred after 1950. The efforts of the High School Board of Education to integrate the community in support of its policy proposals and that community's reactions are the basis of Chapter Two.

[29] David W. Minar, "Democracy in the Suburbs," *Northwestern Tri-Quarterly*, Fall, 1962, pp. 23–28.

# 2 | Social Conflict and Political Integration in New Trier, 1953–63

In urban, suburban, and rural communities throughout the nation, one can find numerous examples of events and policies which have resulted in social conflict. The incidents around which controversy develops vary; it may stem from changes in the structure of political authority in the community, attitudes towards particular individuals or groups, the perception of threats to strongly held cultural values, or attempts to alter the economic structure, especially increased tax rates. James Coleman, in constructing his theory of community conflict, has suggested three common conditions for the development of a controversy from an event: (a) it must affect an important aspect of the residents' lives, (b) it must affect different community members differently, and (c) residents must feel that they are able to do something about the event.[1] Because of their rapid growth and increased social diversification, surburban communities are quite susceptible to controversy, and very often the basis of a particular issue is to be found in the school system.[2]

Two reasons—one quantitative and the other qualitative—may be advanced to explain the high incidence of educationally based social conflict in suburbia. The large

---

[1] James S. Coleman, *Community Conflict* (Glencoe, Ill.: The Free Press, 1957), p. 4.
[2] See the account of social conflict in the Levittown (New York) school system over a school book in Joseph Maloney, *"The Lonesome Train" in Levittown* (University, Ala.: University of Alabama Press, 1958).

number of families with school-age children moving to suburbia makes the provision of public education a prodigious task; providing facilities fast enough to keep pace with school enrollments is a major problem for most suburbs. In the first place, educational expenditures account for between 50 and 75 per cent of every local tax dollar, and the demand for more classrooms and teachers necessitates a never-ending series of tax-rate and bond referenda to increase this percentage. Each of these referenda is a formal invitation to community conflict. Second, the steady stream of new arrivals in the community, as Robert C. Wood has observed, exaggerates whatever social conflict already exists between "native" and newcomer, commuter and local entrepreneur, the young and the old, industrial and residential taxpayer, and various religious and ethnic groups.[3]

There is also a qualitative aspect to the problem of providing adequate public education in the urban fringe communities. The child-oriented suburbanites want more than just adequate education; they demand an educational excellence from the school system that will prepare their children for college, or at least teach them the technical skills necessitated by a modern economy. Indeed, many residents of suburbia have moved there for that very purpose. But since there is no single, precise definition of "educational excellence," the policies of the school board and the administration with regard to curriculum, financing, faculty, and facilities often invite community controversy. The social and political homogeneity of a suburban community often obscures the value differences among its residents; these become manifest only during a controversy. Wood has observed that if you "take the outright quantitative pressures on schools, add the requirements of modern culture, and mix philosophical asser-

[3] Robert C. Wood, *Suburbia: Its People and Politics* (Boston: Houghton Mifflin Co., 1959), p. 187.

tions that cause fundamental issues about human nature, an explosion is inevitable."[4]

Of course, the problems of public education are raised and resolved in different ways in different types of communities, although there is much that is similar from one to another. This chapter is primarily concerned with the social conflict that occurred in a "blue ribbon" community over the attempts of the high school board to expand educational facilities to cope with increased enrollments.

The social and political profile of the New Trier High School District presented in the preceding chapter suggested a community with a relatively homogeneous population, a governmental process specifically designed to avoid overt conflict, and a social credo reading, "Don't rock the boat." But despite these deterrents, a serious social conflict did occur in the New Trier District over school expansion policy.

## The Seeds of Discontent: A $5,000,000 Miscalculation

The open conflict which pervaded the New Trier District in 1961–62 had its genesis in two post–World War II policy decisions made by the Board of Education in response to the pressures of enrollment growth. Despite the fact that district enrollment had steadily decreased during the war and was expected to continue in that direction for several years, Superintendent Gaffney and the Board anticipated the growth that materialized after 1948. Accordingly, in the fall of 1945 an architectural firm was retained to advise the Board in providing for the postwar future of New Trier. After two years of study, a plan was adopted calling for construction of a new music building, demolition of the auditorium and fifty-year-old central tower building, and erection of a new auditorium and a larger classroom-administration structure in

[4] *Ibid.*, p. 189.

that area. The music building was completed in 1950; by that time the upward enrollment trend had begun, and the Board continued its study of the District's needs. A faculty building committee was appointed in the fall of 1951 to work with the Board and administration. Over the next two years this group, in consultation with teachers, parents, and architects, made an extensive examination of New Trier's facilities in relation to its anticipated needs. The main concern was with the ability of New Trier to maintain its level of excellence in the face of expected enrollment increases and of partial obsolescence of the existent plant. A series of studies, interviews, and co-ordinating sessions among the participating groups resulted in five revisions of the Board's original plan. It was ultimately determined that (a) the tower building had classrooms that were too small, corridors that were too narrow, and structural members that were too weak to carry concentrated loads; (b) the auditorium was inadequate; and (c) the heating and electrical systems throughout the plant needed modernization.

As classes began in September, 1953, the Board announced its intention of holding a December referendum to ask voter approval of certain propositions. These would authorize the Board to raze the tower and auditorium, to issue $5,875,000 in bonds to build a new administration-classroom building and an auditorium, and to modernize the heating and electrical systems. Because of the amount of the bond issue, the Board, which in the past had never been overly concerned about gaining community support for its policies, felt that some justification was necessary. In a brochure mailed to every district residence and through publicity in village newspapers, the Board argued that in its judgment, based on seven years of study, the program of expansion to be voted on represented changes necessary "to continue the program of classes and activities that this community wants." It was explained that the older buildings were outmoded and did not provide the space needed; only fourteen of forty-two rooms in the tower building could be used for classes because of warnings issued by the fire marshal. Furthermore, estimated enrollment increases, based on elementary school registrations and reported plans for two new parochial high schools in the township, could be accommodated in the enlarged facilities. The fact that the district was virtually debt-free and that the proposed expansion would cost the taxpayers only $1.00 per $1,000.00 of assessed valuation was also emphasized.

In an attempt to vitiate possible criticism of its program, the Board sought to make it clear that various alternatives to the expansion problem had been considered, including remanding the ninth grade to the elementary schools, and the construction of a second high school. The first was rejected by a joint meeting of the district's elementary school boards in October, 1953, because of the increased burden on their facilities and possible legal restrictions.[5] With regard to a second school, the Board reported that this alternative was seriously considered and then was rejected on two grounds. First, the cost would be extremely high: the architects had estimated that to duplicate the present plant in full would cost $10,850,000 exclusive of site ($1.80 per $1,000.00 assessed valuation), and the cost of a school for 1,500 students would be $7,200,000 plus site cost ($1.25 per $1,000.00 of assessed valuation). In addition, the cost of operating and maintaining a second school would be $951,000 per year. Secondly, there was considerable concern over the "splintering" effect that a second high school in the district would have on the community, fear that the reputation and prestige of the "old" New Trier would not be transferred to the new school, and uncertainty as to whether the smaller second school could offer a suitable variety of educational opportunities.

Despite the Board's efforts, both organized and unorganized opposition to the program developed during the months

[5] See below, p. 56.

before the referendum. Several citizens used the "Public Forum" column of the village newspapers to voice their disapproval of the cavalier fashion with which the Board presented its program; they charged that it failed to give sufficient information to allow intelligent appraisal of the cost involved. They were answered with letters from other residents defending the Board's action, and from Superintendent Gaffney and a Board member supplying such requested data as cost per square foot and cost per pupil, and reiterating that the expense was justified by the community's interest in maintaining New Trier's educational excellence and national reputation.

More opposition to the program developed in the form of the "Committee for Re-equipping the Present New Trier High School and Building a Second High School," organized by three Winnetka residents two weeks prior to the referendum. The committee's position, predicated on the proposition that the $6,000,000 could be better spent on a second school, and the Board's refutation of this position were to have a significant bearing on the 1961–63 campaign for a second New Trier. The committee argued that the Board had not thoroughly explored the alternatives to expanding the existing plant, and asked the voters of the district to reject the referendum propositions authorizing the razing of buildings and issuance of bonds for construction, and to approve only the proposition dealing with modernization of the heating and electrical systems. The committee proposed that a second referendum be held in April, 1954, authorizing renovation of the plant without tearing down buildings, and providing for the construction of a second school. The new school was to reduce the enrollment of the original high school by 1,000 at first, and to have a maximum enrollment of 1,500. The committee stressed the value of "bearing in mind that it is always important to maintain the present high academic standards for both schools, to provide the schools with proper staffs, and to give real consideration to the cost of giving the same facilities to every child anywhere in the district." The Board of Education, which was represented at both meetings of the committee, retorted with its estimates indicating that enrollments were not likely to get unwieldy for a single school and that the pending referendum would provide facilities to meet the needs of the District "for at least the next twenty-five years." The Board reiterated its position regarding the "extravagant" costs of a second school; it also stated its conclusion that "no adequate site" for providing equal services to the students was available in the township, and declared that it would never agree to a second school inferior to the present one. Other objections were listed by the Board: (a) the educational disadvantages of too small a school, (b) the difficulty of getting a favorable vote on the committee's proposal from the entire community, (c) the problems involved in forcing students from fixed geographical areas to attend the new school, (d) the difficulty in finding a centrally located site, and (e) the difficulty in providing equal facilities in buildings, faculty, and reputation.

On December 12, 1953, the voters of the New Trier District approved all five of the Board's propositions by a five-to-two margin in a record turn-out (23 per cent of the eligible voters). Each of the five propositions carried easily in all seven voting precincts. Demolition of the old tower and auditorium was begun during the summer of 1954, and the new buildings, designed to increase the capacity of the high school to 3,000 with provisions for expansion to 3,500, were dedicated in September, 1957. The immediate effect of the referendum was a clear rejection of the alternatives to a single four-year high school in New Trier, particularly the proposal for a second school. But the population growth of the district, which had increased New Trier's enrollment to 3,389 by the time the expanded facilities were dedicated, made it very clear that the issue of expansion would be raised again soon.

## The Growth of Dissatisfaction: The 1957 Debacle

Less than five months after the renovated New Trier campus was dedicated, the Board of Education unexpectedly announced its intention of acquiring a seven-acre area contiguous with the school grounds on the west. This plan culminated in the first referendum defeat ever suffered by a New Trier Board of Education, increased the general dissatisfaction with School Board policy that was aroused in 1953, and had important implications for the events of 1961–63.

On February 28, 1957, the village newspapers of New Trier Township reported that the High School Board had announced plans to acquire twenty-nine homes on seven acres adjacent to the school for use as an intramural athletic field. The Board's position was that increasing enrollment in recent years had made the present athletic grounds inadequate for the kind of physical education and intramural program "deserved by the school and the community and required by state law."[6] It was emphasized that land was last acquired by the District in 1921, when the enrollment was only 1,000; by 1957, the student body had more than tripled, and more space was needed to accommodate its physical-education needs.

Because twenty-nine families and their homes were involved, the Board announced that its program called for "acquisition of additional space with a minimum of inconvenience to those whose homes are involved. The property will be acquired over a period consistent with school needs, estimated at three years." Purchases were to be made from the build-

---

[6] The Illinois School Code, Sec. 27–6, requires that "pupils enrolled in the public schools . . . engage daily, during the school day, in courses of physical education and health instruction . . ." (*The School Code of Illinois*, Circular Series A, No. 146 [Springfield: Office of the Superintendent of Public Instruction, 1961]).

ing-tax fund "in a fair and orderly fashion as the homes come on the market," which meant that a referendum was not contemplated. The announcement concluded with a statement that the Board had already entered into an agreement for one of the homes, and that the entire plan would be the subject of a public meeting at the high school on March 4.

Approximately a hundred residents of the area affected by the Board's expansion plan attended the March 4 meeting and engaged the School Board and Superintendent Cornog in a heated discussion. Among the points raised by the residents were these:

(a) Why hadn't the 1957 Winnetka Caucus meeting, which had convened just a month earlier, been informed of the Board's plans?

(b) How did it "happen" that the first house-purchase agreement was made the day after the announcement of the plan?

(c) How could any of these houses come on the market under "normal conditions" after the publication of the Board's plans? There was only one possible buyer —the School Board.

(d) Was the Board afraid of a District referendum on the plan?

(e) The money available for the purchase of these homes was not sufficient; at least $900,000 plus the cost of demolition and landscaping would be necessary, and the 1957–58 budget allowed only $100,000.

(f) Wasn't the Board being shortsighted? Why not plan beyond the next few years on the basis of population projections, and consider the possibility of a second high school?

The Board defended its policy on pragmatic grounds. Superintendent Cornog maintained that the state of the physical education program at New Trier was a "glaring deficiency" in an otherwise excellent educational system. At the time only 15.5 acres of New Trier's site was available for physical education, and this area would accommodate only 22 per cent of the constantly expanding student body. He said that the rule of thumb used in estimating the necessary land area for a student body is to start with ten acres and add one for each hundred students; based on an enrollment of 4,000, New Trier needed about fifty acres, or almost double the present acreage. It was therefore obvious, said the Board, that more land was needed. The only ways to get it were to condemn it through the power of eminent domain, or to deal directly with the owners of the area involved. It was hoped that the latter course could be pursued, but in either case, there would be some hardship on the families involved; no amount of money, the Board realized, could compensate for the affection one has for his home.

The Board did not consider, and perhaps did not want to consider, that there were alternative sites, unoccupied, for athletic fields in the District; the concept of "one school–one site," firmly established during the tenure of Superintendent Gaffney (1931–54), was decisive in this case. But as a result of the opposition voiced at the March 4 meeting, the Board decided that it would reconsider its expansion proposal. Before the meeting adjourned on March 4, the trustees, declaring that they were still "open-minded" concerning solutions to the problem, scheduled a special meeting of the School Board to consider the opinions expressed by residents. A statement from the Board could be expected within a week.

The threatened homeowners were encouraged by the Board's decision to reconsider, but remained apprehensive. One night later (March 5), those affected, joined by other District residents who were alarmed at the Board's proposed action, met to discuss the situation. The stated consensus of the group was that, while they were very much concerned with the welfare of the school and with maintaining its high standards, the estimated cost of converting their seven acres into intramural fields—$170,000 per acre—led them to believe that the Board should consider the problem from a long-term perspective. In other words, wouldn't the seven acres prove to be only an expensive stopgap?

The Board of Education met on March 11 and announced that, after careful re-examination of the property-acquisition question, the Board's original proposal had been reaffirmed. It added that a referendum would be held on this question, but no date was set and no details were given.

One month later (on April 8), the Board's intentions were clarified. A bond referendum—estimated, pending property appraisal, at $900,000—would be held on June 8, 1957, to provide sufficient funds for the purchase of the seven-acre site. It was reported that one home had been bought and negotiations with about half of the affected owners had been initiated. The Board emphasized that it planned to continue its efforts to acquire the acreage *regardless of the referendum outcome*; the only question to be decided by the referendum was whether the tract was to be purchased out of building-tax levies or from the proceeds from the sale of bonds.

By May 2, the Board's attitude toward the upcoming referendum had been challenged. An *ad hoc* group known as the New Trier Taxpayers' Committee was organized by four Winnetkans because they felt that the District electorate should be given the opportunity to vote on the "basic question": Should the Board acquire the seven acres? In response to letters sent to "representative citizens" of the New Trier community, fifty residents met to discuss the Board's proposal and possible ways of expressing their dissatisfaction with it. It was decided to attempt to force a "basic question" referendum in the District, as authorized by the Illinois school and election codes; the Board was required to hold such a referendum upon petition of 25 per cent of the registered District voters.

Although cautioned that such action should be taken under only the most unusual circumstances, since, after all, the Board of Education must be relied on for all policy decisions not included in the referendum (i.e., "Don't antagonize the Board"), the committee resolved to go to the voters with a six-point case:

(a) The Board had made a major break with past District policy. In the first place, it had replaced the 3,000-student school concept with a 5,000-student school concept, which would create new problems of assimilating eighth-graders, of parking, and of transportation. Secondly, the "good neighbor" policy of all past School Boards had been repudiated with a plan to force 150 people from twenty-nine homes. During the 1953 expansion campaign, for instance, the Board, when questioned about acquiring land adjoining the campus, had replied that this was neither "economic nor neighborly"; what had occurred in the past four years to make this plan economic and neighborly? Third, and perhaps most significant, the Board was attempting to bar township voters from expressing any opinion except on the method of payment. The purchase of the first home in the tract had been "shrouded in secrecy," and the 1957 Winnetka Caucus had not been informed of the Board's contemplated action. "It is a mockery to say you may vote on a bond issue but if you vote it down, we are going ahead anyway."

(b) The cost of the tract was outlandish. Appraisers had indicated the cost would be $1,000,000–$1,100,000 for acquisition and $100,000 to prepare the land for school use—or about $160,000 per acre. This was a "fantastic" price to pay for a supplemental playfield area, which due to cold weather could be used only a few weeks before and after summer vacations.

(c) The Board's position on the destruction of twenty-nine homes was "weak and indefensible." The Board had argued that acquisition of adjacent land in 1945, 1947, and 1953, when it was previously considered, was "not appropriate" because of the housing shortage and the need for more buildings on the campus, but now contended that it was "both necessary and proper." But was it? No physical education classes were ever held on the football field, which was used at most only four or five Saturdays a year; possible damage to the turf hardly justified the expenditure of $1,100,000 or the expulsion of twenty-nine families from their homes.

(d) The purchase of these seven acres was only a stopgap measure. By the Board's own admission, the current 15.5 acres of playfield accomodated only 22 per cent of the student body. These figures indicated that 75 acres were needed for the present enrollment and that projected increases would necessitate even more. It was obvious, therefore, that seven acres was not sufficient for school needs.

(e) The Board had misrepresented the physical education requirements of Illinois state law. The law required only that 200 minutes per week be spent in physical education classes, without stipulating outdoor activity. New Trier High School's gyms and fieldhouse were more than adequate for this purpose. Furthermore, the minutes of a recent Board meeting indicated that inadequate locker space, not outdoor space, was limiting girls' physical education.

(f) *If* the problem was acute, there were better solutions. One might be to reduce the size of the District, which had expanded beyond its original boundaries. A more satisfactory solution would be the construction of a second high school campus in the District. Five districts in Cook County had built or were building second campuses. The County Superintendent of Public Instruction considered a student body of 2,000–3,000 ideal; New Trier was approaching 4,000, and expectations were that the figure would go even higher.

The committee also expressed a desire to discuss the issue with Superintendent Cornog in an open meeting, but it was reported that committee organizers had had little co-operation from the Board or administration thus far.

Superintendent Cornog and the School Board became apprehensive. Cornog arranged to address the Wilmette Rotary Club, and both he and the Board president were scheduled to speak to a joint meeting of the Kenilworth school board and its parents' organization on the subject of the upcoming referendum.

On May 6, five members of the New Trier Taxpayers' Committee, representing Wilmette, Glencoe, and Winnetka, met with the Board of Education and Superintendent Cornog in an attempt to avert an open conflict. Instead, the positions of both sides were reaffirmed. The Board stated that it had "investigated the matter thoroughly, and that its action was best for all concerned"; it would proceed with the June 8 referendum as planned. Simultaneously, it announced that a letter presenting the Board's views on the matter would be mailed to all households in the District within a few days. Further, "in order to bring details of the whole question to the attention of all the voters in the township, and to provide an opportunity to answer all questions," a series of public meetings with civic and educational groups throughout the District was being scheduled.

The committee's position was also restated in much the same terms as previously: The voters have a right to an answer to the basic question at issue—that of whether the Board should buy the seven-acre tract. School expansion is an important decision, involving all citizens, their children, and their tax money, and an opportunity should be afforded to vote "yes" or "no" on the question. It was reported that petitions calling for a "basic question" referendum were circulating throughout the District. They had also been placed with merchants and would be mailed to every home. All residents of the District, whether for or against the June 8 referendum, would be urged by the committee to sign the petitions in order to get an answer to the "basic question."

During the next few weeks each side endeavored to put its case before the people. The Board's letter to District residents stressed the need for additional acreage, the Board's responsibility for making the decision whether to acquire the property in question or not, and the irrelevancy of the second high school issue to the present question. It was pointed out, however, that the Board and administration were considering the possibility of a second school, and had decided "to engage experts to re-survey population trends and all possible sites as a basis for continuing study of the situation." In addition, Board members and Superintendent Cornog defended their position before scheduled group meetings throughout the District; and, one week before the referendum, the Executive Committee of the New Trier Parents' Association supported the Board in a letter mailed to all parents.

The Taxpayers' Committee avoided further direct contact with the Board, but proceeded on two fronts. Efforts to obtain the necessary petition signatures were continued in earnest, and, on May 23, a full-page ad appeared in each of the Lloyd Hollister newspapers published weekly in the villages of the District:

> Let's make our High School tax money work for us; we work hard enough for it. Why should New Trier High School spend $200,000 per acre for seven acres when this money would buy twenty times as much land elsewhere while still

available? Such land would accommodate some intramural and all interscholastic sports and would be available for a second campus if New Trier decided to follow this modern concept to avoid having a city-type high school.

Seven acres will only accommodate 308 students, at a cost of $1,400,000. Should this high sum be spent for such insignificant benefits? Now is the time to buy vacant land before the size of the school, the ultimate cost, and the problems become insurmountable.

Opposed to acquisition or not, insist on your right to vote; sign a petition for a referendum as authorized by state school law. Vote "NO"

In the issue preceding the June 8 referendum, the Hollister papers took an editorial stand which might be construed as an endorsement of the Board's view. The editorial writer maintained that too many extraneous issues had been injected. Although he was of the opinion that New Trier was getting too large, and the solution appeared to be a second school, the future growth of the high school was quite beside the point; that issue would have to be resolved separately, and should have no bearing on this referendum.

A new turn-out record was set on June 8 when 27 per cent of the eligible District voters rejected the New Trier Board's proposal, by 6,644 to 1,549. The $900,000 bond issue failed to carry a single precinct, and received less than 30 per cent of the vote in all but one.

In view of the overwhelming lack of confidence indicated by this vote, the Board rescinded its February resolution and discontinued *all* efforts to purchase the tract. It announced, however, that it would seek land away from the school to which interscholastic activities could be transferred. A long-range survey of District population trends would also be made to inform future District planning.

In the light of the Board's decision, the New Trier Taxpayers' Committee ceased its efforts to force a "basic issue" referendum, and praised the Board for its action, which it asserted reflected "the conscientious attitude of the Board." An effort to heal social wounds caused by the committee's opposition was apparent from published comments by the committee members:

> We are certain that the residents of the District will close ranks and unite in an effort to maintain, and if possible, improve the high educational standards that New Trier enjoys. We would like to find something concerning the school that we can work for as diligently as we worked against this in the past.[7]

Eventually, the Board did manage to get additional playground space on a site that was to figure importantly in the 1961 and 1962 site referenda. In July, 1959, it was announced that the New Trier Board, the Winnetka park board, and the village council of Winnetka had reached agreement on a lease-sale deal for 47 acres in western Winnetka owned by that village. The park and high school boards had submitted competing bids for this land in 1958. The village council, apparently not wanting to make a decision, suggested that the two boards develop plans for joint use of recreational facilities on the site. The agreement provided that 10 acres, then used by Winnetka as a sanitary-fill area, be sold to New Trier High School for $80,000, with the stipulation that Winnetka use it for fill until it was full. This site was to be used eventually for a new stadium. Of the remaining 37 acres, the high school leased 18.5 for eighteen years. No structures would be permitted on this land, which was intended for use as varsity athletic practice fields by the high school to release space at the campus for intramural athletics. However, the agreement was held in abeyance, pending an advisory referendum to be submitted to the Winnetka electorate on October 10, 1959.

Aside from a plea to Winnetkans, citing the "urgent need" for space to expand its physical education program, the High School Board did little or nothing in the way of

[7] *Wilmette Life,* June 13, 1957.

campaigning. On October 10, 11 per cent of the Winnetka electorate approved the sale-lease agreement by better than two to one (653–272); the proposition failed to carry in only two of fifteen precincts, both adjacent to the site.

Thus, two years after its ignominious first referendum defeat and its subsequent policy retreat, the School Board had found a temporary alternative solution to the immediate problem of enrollment increase and lack of space. But the long-range problem of increasing high school enrollments could not be resolved by the acquisition of athletic fields. More serious expansion difficulties were to develop.

## A Shift in School Board Policy: The 1961 Decision to Build a Second High School

The Board of Education had "promised," during the 1957 campus-expansion campaign, to have experts conduct a population-projection study of the District as a basis for continued evaluation of expansion alternatives. This promise was honored when the University of Chicago's Department of Education submitted its report in December, 1957. The Board was lulled into inaction by the figures. Based on the potential of the two new Catholic high schools being built in the District, the experts' predicted enrollment peak for New Trier High School was only 4,250; this would be 827 less than Assistant Superintendent Wesley Brown's January, 1957, projection (5,077), and only 861 higher than the enrollment at the time (3,389).

But by November, 1960, when Assistant Superintendent Brown submitted a re-estimate of the high school enrollment peak based on detailed and extensive analysis of elementary enrollments, it was apparent that the University of Chicago projection would be quickly and considerably exceeded. At that time, the enrollment had already increased to 3,902 and showed no signs of peaking in the near future. Brown's new data and analysis pointed toward a peak of 5,164 in 1968, which would decrease to 5,054 when residential construction in the District reached a saturation point in 1973.[8] This information was published in the Hollister papers on December 1, 1960, but it brought forth no immediate reaction.[9]

In his November 10 report to the Board, Brown pointed out that New Trier's enrollment then exceeded the intended capacity of the school by more than 400. Class size had been increased to accommodate these students, and it could be increased further, but only at the risk of reducing educational quality; such measures should be temporary. Brown, apparently with the concurrence of Superintendent Cornog, expressed the opinion that it was not a question of *whether* or not to build more facilities; the major question to be answered by the Board was *where* to build and *for whom*. Five alternatives were suggested, each of which had major advantages and disadvantages:

(a) add buildings on the present site to accommodate 1,200 additional students;

(b) contract with the elementary school districts to retain the ninth-graders in their junior high schools;

(c) build a 1,300-student school for the ninth grade only on another site;

(d) construct a second four-year high school (to be known as New Trier High School West) on another site for 1,500 students, and apportion the district;

(e) build a 2,600-student school on another site for grades nine and ten and use the present plant for grades eleven and twelve, and for a junior college.[10]

[8] Wesley Brown, "A Prediction of Maximum Enrollment After Building Saturation for New Trier Township High School District" (17 pp., mimeo.; New Trier Township High School, Nov. 10, 1960).

[9] One fairly reliable indicator of community reaction is the number and tone of letters published in the "Public Forum" column of the Hollister papers. Letters concerning New Trier are published in all the papers.

[10] Brown, "A Prediction . . . ," p. 14.

Although decision and action were imperative if serious overcrowding was to be averted, the Brown Report cautioned the Board to conduct a "careful study and complete discussion of all the possible solutions by as many of the responsible people of this school district as can be involved." The following approach was recommended:

As a first step, all of the possible solutions to the problem, including those mentioned above, should be assembled. Each solution should be studied exhaustively and the advantages and disadvantages of that solution listed.

After each study it will become apparent that some of the alternatives should be discarded. At this point, all but the two most favored solutions should be discarded and further exhaustive study be given to a choice between the remaining two solutions. All factors should be weighed, but major emphasis should be given to reasons for action which lead towards the best possible educational outcome.

By law, the New Trier Township High School Board of Education must make the final decision, but such a complete study of possibilities as here proposed should be very helpful. Obviously, complete publicity should be given to this study so that all of the voters of the township shall be kept informed as to the reasoning involved.

It is inevitable that there shall be discussion, proposal, and counter-proposal. However, the best outcome will be achieved if all of this occurs before a final decision is made and before the electorate is asked to vote on this decision. The best thinking of the Parents Association, the elementary school boards of education, and all interested citizens is solicited.[11]

It was pointed out that regardless of the choice made from among the stated alternatives, providing facilities for 1,300 or more additional students would be expensive. Brown estimated that a second high school, the alternative which had been strongly supported by Board opponents during both the 1953 and 1957 expansion campaigns, would cost between $4,000,000 and $5,000,000 (for 1,300–1,500 students) includ-

11 *Ibid.*, p. 15.

ing site. Bonding power, limited to 5 per cent of the District's assessed valuation, was more than adequate regardless of the alternative chosen—that is, it was $17,500,000 less the $3,600,000 in bonds outstanding (as of 1961).

The Hollister papers reported the alternatives being considered by the School Board on December 8, 1960, and related that a decision was expected by early spring. Again no immediate public reaction was discernible.

One week later, a report by Cornog and Brown reviewing the pros and cons of each proposal, and designed only as a "guide to stimulate thinking on the subject," was submitted to the Board of Education.[12] This report held that the first and basic question to be answered was whether there should be one or two sites:

> The proposition which faces us is whether it is better to enlarge our present school, which now has enrolled 3900 and is approximately full, or to do additional building on some other site, giving us one school of 3500 to 3800 and a second school of 1300 to 1700. To have less than 3500 in our present building would be an uneconomical use of it. The present school plant is valued at over $14,000,000. It provides as closely as is possible what is best in secondary school education. It is located near the center of the district. Traditionally, boys and girls from all over the present district have come here. A second school would be about half the size of this school. It would have to compare favorably in quality. It will be difficult to find a site appropriately located without a major expenditure for site alone. It may be difficult to draw natural boundaries for such a school, and it is probable that a considerable percentage of parents and students included in such boundaries will be opposed to the idea of a second school.[13]

Among the reasons for adding to the existing site cited in the report were the relatively low cost that would be made

[12] William Cornog and Wesley Brown, "A Cursory Examination of the Several Proposals for Additional New Trier Township High School Building" (5 pp., mimeo.; New Trier Township High School, Dec. 15, 1960).

[13] *Ibid.*, p. 1.

possible by avoiding facility duplication; a greater flexibility of curriculum; and an increased variety of courses and services. Disadvantages of this solution included the aggravation of traffic and parking problems around the school; increased tension and fatigue for both faculty and students as a result of more complex organization; and the difficulties of working with the extremely small site (twenty-seven acres) on which the present school was located.

Of the four second-site proposals, the four-year school was the one most often discussed. In its favor were its smaller enrollment (1,500–1,200), its proximity to its students' homes, and the additional opportunities for leadership and extracurricular activities it would create. The major drawbacks were its high cost (duplication of expensive facilities like a pool and auditorium) and the difficulty of drawing attendance boundaries satisfactory to the entire community.

Remanding the ninth grade to elementary-district junior highs presupposed an arrangement between the high school and each of the six elementary districts. Such an arrangement is provided for by Illinois law, but it has never been used, and its practicality and constitutionality were doubted.[14] In addition, the statute specifically provides only for the high school to compensate the elementary districts for the "maintenance and operation" of the junior high, and does not mention capital expenditures; it was considered doubtful that the elementary districts had sufficient bonding power to provide the necessary additional facilities, or the desire to pay for and administer them. It was also possible that building facilities at six separate locations would be more expensive than building one ninth-grade school on a new site.

The latter alternative, although it had the advantage of providing a transitional year from junior high to high school, presented serious problems of faculty staffing, because few teachers like to teach only one grade.

[14] School Code, Sec. 13–10.

The final proposal considered by the Board was the construction of a freshman-sophomore school on a new site and a junior-senior high school plus junior college in the present building. This was the most expensive plan; and, in any case, there was little support for a publicly financed junior college in the New Trier community.

The superintendent and his assistant felt that an "essential concord of opinion" should be established in the community before a final decision was made from among these five alternatives. Wide publicity and open discussion of the total question would, they hoped, achieve such consensus prior to a bond election.

During January, the Board met weekly to examine the educational values and the costs of the various alternatives, so that a decision could be made no later than the end of February. In the same period, Cornog met with the elementary school boards and administrative staffs to discuss the alternatives. The public knew what these alternatives were, but neither "wide publicity" nor "open discussion" ever materialized. The public was merely informed through the local press that the Board's decision would be based on "all the information and professional opinion" the Board could summon, and that the proposal selected would be the one thought best calculated to maintain education in New Trier at a quality second to none.

On February 20, 1961, the School Board unanimously made its official decision, and the February 23 editions of the Hollister papers relayed it to the public. Convinced that the unique qualities of a New Trier education could best be preserved through two four-year high schools, the Board had chosen to build a second school for 1,700 to 2,000 students on a site in Northfield consisting of thirty (subsequently increased to forty-five) acres. The Board said its decision had been reached only after an intensive study, in which it was assisted by faculty, students, elementary-district trustees and staffs, and a committee of the New Trier Parents' Association. The cost of both the site and the construction of the school were to be announced prior to the site referendum. This solution, said the Board, would maintain close student-faculty relationships, increase extracurricular opportunities, and provide a safeguard in the event of unforeseen population growth.

The following week, additional information concerning the decision was announced. The referendum was to be held in late May or early June. To allay parental fears, the Board made it clear that no student presently enrolled in New Trier would be affected by the decision, that there would be an equitable distribution of teachers and staff between both schools, and that the second school would be "fully compara-ble" and under the same administration as the present school. Furthermore, in order to answer questions and attempt to win the support of community residents, the Board, in co-operation with parents' organizations, scheduled public meetings in elementary districts throughout the High School District.

On March 23, it was announced that the public meetings on the new school—to be called New Trier West in order to preserve the "New Trier" label—would be held between April 24 and May 18. In addition to the six elementary school meetings, the Board also planned to meet with three influential civic groups in the community—Wilmette Rotary, Winnetka Lions, and Glenayre Property Owners' Association—and to conclude with a general meeting at the high school. At each meeting the Board planned to present the second-school proposal and answer questions, a strategy calcu-lated to communicate intent, and presumably to generate consensus.

Before the meetings began, the site bond referendum was scheduled for May 20, and the amount of the bond was set at $975,000 (for forty-five acres). In rapid succession, the cost of

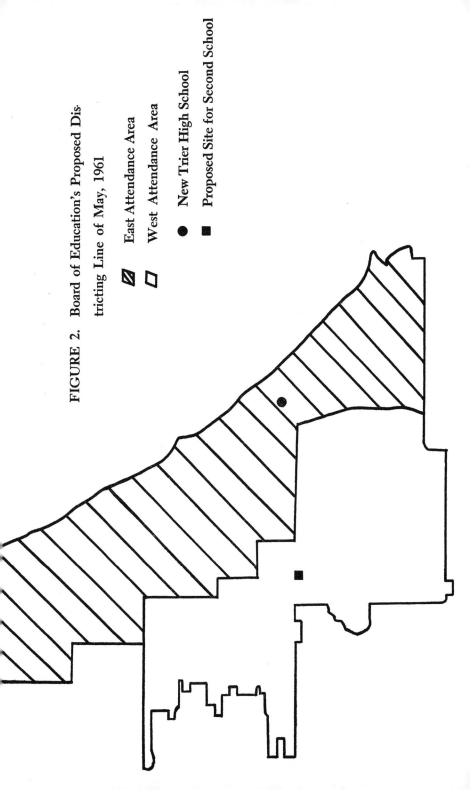

FIGURE 2. Board of Education's Proposed Districting Line of May, 1961

East Attendance Area

West Attendance Area

● New Trier High School

■ Proposed Site for Second School

building the new school was announced to be an estimated $7,500,000, for which approval would be sought in the fall, and the tentative enrollment districting was publicized. Residents of the Avoca and Sunset Ridge elementary districts (Northfield and unincorporated areas) and the western section of the Wilmette school district (west Wilmette and Glenview) would "probably" attend the new school (see Figure 2).

The effect of this series of Board decisions, and the districting one in particular, on parts of the community were immediate and lasting. Within several days, the School Board's scheduled meeting in the Sunset Ridge school district was held. It was attended by over 250 residents, and it lasted three hours; certain statements made during the evening initiated an inter-village controversy that was *a* major, if not *the* major, factor in the referendum defeat in May.

Northfielders vociferously opposed the trustees' decision regarding the new school. They objected on two grounds—location and districting. In the first place, they argued that it was much too expensive for a small village like Northfield to bear the original and continuing costs of a high school.[15] Other sites in the District, notably in Wilmette, were suggested to the Board. These included a golf course in west Wilmette owned by Northwestern University and a farm in south-central Wilmette. Could it be, suggested one resident, that a Northfield site was selected because the village was too small to fight back and defeat a referendum?

The School Board, obviously in hostile territory, attempted to defend the site decision. Loring Farwell, Northfield's representative on the Board, contended that, since there was no other "suitable" site in the township, the

---

[15] It was estimated that, in addition to one-time expenditures such as street widening and sewer installation, it would cost Northfield $25,000 per year to host the new school because of the additional fire and police equipment and personnel that would be needed.

school must be located in Northfield. All other sites in the District had been carefully considered and were found wanting, with the possible exception of a site within the Cook County Forest Preserve, but this was not available. Concerning the expense, the Board was quick to point out that the construction of a new high school was a District-wide problem, and the costs would be proportioned among the several villages.

Northfield's second objection concerned the quality of education that would result from the Board's districting decision. According to an unidentified Northfield village trustee's interpretation of the "sense of the meeting," Northfielders felt their children would receive a "poorer education" than was available at the present school, because the children from west Wilmette (who would constitute about 50 per cent of the new student body) had "lower cultural and social aspirations."[16] This fear of unequal educational quality was justified, residents argued, by two "facts": (a) students moving from west Wilmette to Northfield required summer school in order to catch up, and (b) college admissions offices would not accept graduates from New Trier West as readily as from the present school. Superintendent Cornog sharply challenged the latter point, and Trustee Farwell expressed his opinion that, since the distribution of talent was even throughout the District, it was improbable that there could be an unequal distribution of educational quality.

But Northfield's fears were not allayed by the Board's statements, and its citizens remained resolutely opposed to a second school in their village. Making the Board's task more difficult were the repercussions which the Northfield meeting had in west Wilmette. The Hollister papers' report of the proceedings quoted the "cultural and social aspirations" statement out of context, creating the impression that this was in fact the expressed sentiment of those in attendance rather

[16] *Wilmette Life*, April 27, 1961.

than the interpretation of one village official. Somewhat later a letter, written by the chairman of the meeting and questioning the Hollister report, appeared in the "Public Forum" column of the papers; an inconspicuous clarification was then printed, but only after the damage had been done.[17]

The reaction from west Wilmette, whose population is largely Jewish, was immediate. Considerable anger was directed at the residents of Northfield. In a steady stream of letters to the "Public Forum," comments such as the following appeared:

> Northfield is worried about college admissions because of the "social and cultural aspirations" of west Wilmette's children. If they pay more attention to scholastic aspirations than social ones, they will have no problems.

> I sense a plot by the "solid burgers" of east Wilmette, Kenilworth, Winnetka and Glencoe to provide "separate but equal" facilities for those of us who have sought refuge in west Wilmette from the ghettos of Chicago. Vote "no"! One Township, one high school.

> I am opposed to submitting my child to an atmosphere of subterfuge, prejudice and "social" tension in a Northfield school. Districting must be resolved more satisfactorily; I do not like an east-west split of the District without including all villages. A freshman-sophomore school would be more democratic.

> The statement made in Northfield has created a dangerous situation. It was an unsound, biased statement and not a credit to their community.

> The real issue in this referendum is segregation. There should be a proportionate representation of *all* villages in the new school. This is more democratic and in keeping with our American way of life. Don't build a wall around west Wilmette.

A few letters from Northfielders indicated remorse over the so-called "Northfield incident" and attempted to mitigate its adverse effect on intercommunity relations. Said one:

[17] *Wilmette Life*, May 4, 1961.

Districting is immaterial since the intelligence level is the same in all villages. West Wilmette students and parents are every bit as good as Northfield's. An apology is due for any insinuation to the contrary.

And another:

The price of the Northfield site includes . . . the cost in community relations. The "social aspirations" statement hurt and piled hurt upon hurt. No governing body or citizenry can expend human relations without risk of injury to the entire community.

There is no indication that any other efforts were made to restore amicable relations between the citizenry of the two communities.

Meanwhile, the Board of Education continued its scheduled series of public meetings, where less volatile but still very important issues were raised. For instance, at the Kenilworth meeting on May 1, Superintendent Cornog answered a charge first made at the Northfield meeting, that college admissions officers would discriminate against New Trier West. He reported that he had telephoned Harvard University's admissions officer recently, and was told that "someone" from the township had called and had unsuccessfully tried to get a statement that Harvard would favor New Trier East graduates over those of a second high school.

At the May 10 Wilmette meeting, Cornog answered questions concerning the Board's districting proposal. It was designed, said the superintendent, to afford the most effective student guidance by keeping junior high school graduating classes intact in high school. Previously proposed changes in the attendance lines involved a division of the District to include parts of all villages in both schools, without regard for the splintering effect on eighth-grade graduating classes.

In the May 11 editions of the Hollister papers, School Board President Marshall Long explained why other sites in the District had been rejected, and the one in Northfield selected for the second school. Once it had been decided that a second high school was the best solution for maintaining a "New Trier type of education," the Board established five criteria to be met in selecting a site: (a) it must be in the southern half of the District, where over 50 per cent of the students resided; (b) it must comprise at least thirty-five acres; (c) it must be accessible, by as many roads as possible, to the area to be served; (d) it must be substantially unimproved, in order to keep costs down; and (e) it must be readily available. Of all the sites considered by the Board, only the Northfield site at Happ and Winnetka roads met the requirements of location, size, accessibility, cost, and availability. It was the "best site available" in the Board's opinion.

With only a week remaining until the referendum, two residents (one from Winnetka, who became the 1962 Democratic candidate for Congress in the Thirteenth District, and one from Wilmette), sensing growing dissatisfaction among the voters over the Board's program, called a "protest" meeting to marshal negative votes. Only fifty people attended, half of whom favored the referendum proposal, and half of whom felt "confused" by the whole thing. The organizers of the meeting criticized the Board soundly for holding public discussion meetings *after* the decisions were made, and for not supplying the public with sufficient information on which to base an intelligent vote. The electorate was advised to defeat the referendum for "want of information"—to vote "no" and wait for the answers. Two advantages to this plan were cited. The public would be better informed, and there would be wider support of the Board's program, whatever it might be. But, it was pointed out, there would also be disadvantages. Land values might rise, increasing the cost of a site, and a defeat could be interpreted as a vote of "no confidence" in the Board. The sponsors of the meeting indicated they would support a package referendum (site and building) in the fall *if* the Board satisfactorily answered all unanswered questions.

In an editorial two days prior to the May 20 referendum, the Hollister papers, main communication channel between the Board and the public, took a noncommittal position. They did little more than point out the obvious: that this was a proposal of "major concern" to every resident of the District, that taxes would probably increase if the referendum were approved, and that the issue was whether the students would get a better education in one large or two smaller high schools. A Hollister editor later admitted that, although the papers had supported the referendum, their stand was less than enthusiastic. "We felt that the New Trier Board of Education had made a real mess of the proposal and the way it was presented; it would be tough to put it over."[18]

Just how tough became clear on May 20. For the third consecutive time, a voting turn-out record for a referendum was set; of an estimated 36,200 eligible voters in the District, 11,907 (33 per cent) cast ballots. The referendum was defeated 6,675–5,232, marking the second rejection in four years of a major School Board expansion proposal.

## Another Attempt: Communication, Co-optation, and Community Integration in 1962

The New Trier Board of Education was momentarily stunned by the community's rejection of its solution to the expansion crisis. Since the Board had determined that a second school on the Northfield site was the most education-ally sound solution to a pressing community problem, it had therefore assumed that this measure would be accepted by a large plurality. After all, with the exception of the 1957 refer-endum defeat, for which the Board itself had accepted respon-sibility, that was the way things were done in the District. The reasons for this defeat were no clearer to the community at large than they were to the Board. Did defeat signify rejection

[18] Interview with the editor of the *Wilmette Life,* November 6, 1962.

of the second-school concept, the Northfield site, or the relatively high cost of the land ($22,000 per acre)?

To evaluate the failure of the proposal to win public support and to plan the next move, a special Board meeting was called two days later. In addition to the Board members and administrative staff, reporters from two Chicago newspapers which thought the defeat significant and seventeen residents attended. Two general conclusions were reached after considerable discussion, including the solicitation of opinions from the audience: (a) the Board had failed to communicate effectively with the public in making known the problem and the basis for the decision made to solve it, and (b) the need for action in the matter was urgent. It was suggested that the whole problem be thoroughly restudied, and that the voters be fully informed during the process. Specific plans were offered for informing the Board of community opinion as to a proper solution. These ranged from holding small, informal group meetings in homes throughout the township to having a door-to-door poll conducted by the League of Women Voters. One opponent of Board procedure in attendance that night felt that this change in attitude marked the turning point in the campaign. "Up to then," she said, "the Board was of the opinion that if it *told* us enough times what it had decided to do, the community would buy it; for the first time, they're going to *ask* us."[19]

At the next Board meeting (June 5), Winnetka member Charles Kaufman reported that information he had gathered since the defeat indicated four reasons for the adverse public reaction:

(a) The Board's approach did not include making full information available to the public; decision before discussion on such an important issue was resented.

[19] Interview with Mrs. Francis Hall (Winnetka), October 30, 1962.

(b) The Board's decision to expand the present campus in 1953, made on the basis of facts then known, created distrust of the Board's decisions.

(c) Some citizens thought the cost of the Northfield site was excessive.

(d) Many were alienated by what they felt was a "social-snobbish" attitude on the part of some other residents; it was felt that the new school would have a "different" economic and religious life than old New Trier.

A subcommittee of four trustees (two from Winnetka and one each from Wilmette and Glencoe) was appointed to recommend a procedure for restudying the solution.

On June 19, the Board met to consider the subcommittee's report. As a means of enhancing public understanding, the subcommittee recommended, and the full Board unanimously approved, a plan to establish a citizens' advisory committee composed of approximately twenty-five members; the membership would be apportioned among the villages according to the number of homesites in each. The Board would select the committee from names recommended by civic leaders throughout the district, including village officials, elementary school board members, and parents. Four qualifications were set for membership: objectivity, reasonableness, availability, and status in the community.

The task of the citizens' committee would be to review and evaluate all the alternative solutions to the expansion problem (including the original proposition) and make recommendations by November 1, 1961. Superintendent Cornog was sure that the committee could not come up with anything but the "best educational proposal" because it would have all the facts. Nonetheless, because some trustees felt the Board of Education had the responsibility for the ultimate decision, the recommendations of the committee would *not* be binding.

Over two hundred nominations were made by civic leaders, and on July 5 the Board quickly reached agreement on the twenty-six who would make up the Citizens' Study Committee (CSC) and assist the Board "to find the best educational solution to the New Trier population problem."[20] A meeting with the committee was scheduled for July 18. In addition, the Board directed Assistant Superintendent Brown to update his 1960 population study, and authorized trustee Myers to negotiate with the architectural firm of Perkins and Will to act as consultants to both the Board and the CSC.

At the joint School Board–CSC organizational meeting of July 18, it was mutually agreed that, with the exception of administrative assistance and specific requests for information, the committee would be free from any Board influence.[21] The Board then administered the election of committee officers and left. Robert Liebenow (Wilmette), president of the Chicago Board of Trade, was elected chairman—probably, he felt, because he "knew more people on the committee than anyone else." Peter Frielich, a Northfield village trustee and Loop insurance executive, became the vice-chairman. Edward Bullard, a former president of the Winnetka board of education, was voted second vice-chairman. Mrs. R. H. Alschuler, a Glencoe housewife active in the League of Women Voters and a member of the Glencoe board of education, was selected as secretary. The officers then appointed chairmen and members to five subcommittees (costs, site, population, educational standards, and publicity) on the basis of members' personal experience and geographical representation among and within villages. It was decided that the full

[20] Minutes, New Trier Board of Education meeting, July 5, 1961.

[21] In an interview on November 2, 1962, the former CSC chairman told the author: "Our only contact with the Board after that was in the nature of informational inquiries, requests for legal opinions from the school attorney, architectural data, etc. I kept [Superintendent] Cornog informed, and [Board President] Long knew what we were doing by the nature of the requests. But we were completely on our own; there was an atmosphere of complete freedom."

committee would convene twice a month starting August 1, and the subcommittees would meet as often as necessary.

On August 10, the Hollister press reported that Scott, Foresman and Company, a publishing firm, had purchased twenty-five acres of the forty-five acre Northfield site at a cost per acre almost double the $22,000 the Board had planned to spend. A change in zoning of the area from residential to light industrial, approved by the Northfield village council after the May referendum defeat, was cited as the reason such a purchase had been possible. President Long said the Board's position was not altered by this development; the Board would continue to consider *all* expansion alternatives, including the Northfield site.

After six weeks of preliminary discussion and review by the CSC, its population subcommittee recommended that a professional study and projection of student population be made. The greatest part of the committee's recommendations would be influenced by projected growth rates and the subcommittee thought that these should be as accurate as possible. The large difference between the 1957 University of Chicago figures and the 1960 Brown Report was cited as evidence of the need for professional study.

A request for funds was made to the School Board in mid-September, and $4,500 was appropriated for the purpose. Within a week, the Real Estate Research Corporation (RERC) was engaged to make a study of population trends in the district projected to 1980. The RERC report was to be completed by mid-October. In the meanwhile, the CSC would pursue its study in other areas.

While the Board and the CSC set about to find an acceptable solution, the opinion of the community as expressed in the "Public Forum" column indicated what a difficult task they would have. Everyone seemed to agree that a problem existed and that it was acute, but there was little or no agreement on a solution. It also became clear that the May referendum vote had not even settled the one-campus-versus-two question.

The initial public reaction was a plea to put differences aside and work together with the Board to find the best answer to a common problem, in order to preserve the quality of the educational system before it was too late. Soon individual expressions of pet solutions based on a variety of reasons dominated the column—enlarge the old school, put the ninth grade in junior highs, build a freshman school, and so on. In most cases, the solution offered by the letter writer was designed to maximize the benefit to the children of his or her village.

This tendency was most clearly exemplified in an exchange of public letters initiated by an outspoken Northfield resident in mid-August. Citing the cost per acre that Scott, Foresman and Company had paid for twenty-five acres of the Northfield site, Jeremy Beman argued that, since the Board had grossly underestimated the cost of the site, the $7,000,000 estimated cost of a second school might also be low. Using the Board's 1953 figures and allowing for increased building costs, he submitted that the cost would be closer to $13,000,000, which would burden the taxpayers unnecessarily. Without giving his source, he quoted (from the 1960 Cornog-Brown Report) Superintendent Cornog's favorable comments on construction of a freshman school. Beman emphasized the lower cost ($4,000,000) of this proposal and the fact that all students would be given an "equal shake," i.e., would go to the same schools. "Our tax burdens are heavy enough without a $13 million school once rejected when our own Superintendent says that a freshman school is educationally feasible. The world has trouble enough without splitting the District wide open and voting people out of a school with traditions, reputation, and physical plant the result of a half-century."[22]

[22] *Wilmette Life*, August 17, 1961.

A former president of the Winnetka League of Women Voters who was active in school affairs replied the following week. In the first place, she said, Beman had quoted Cornog out of context, because in the report he also gave arguments against a freshman school. Secondly, she felt that, although as a taxpayer she found a freshman school appealing, as a parent she did not. It would be more difficult to attract and keep first-rate teachers under such an arrangement, and the curriculum would lose its flexibility.

Beman's rebuttal followed a week later, giving the source of his Cornog quotation and reiterating the advantages of a freshman school. "We don't need a 13 million dollar Rolls Royce when we can have a 4 million dollar Cadillac. Are we to ignore the mandate of the voters of last Spring? Have the Board give us an alternative of equal benefit to all in the Township."

This exchange attracted other opinions. Another Northfielder reported that he had read the Cornog-Brown Report as a result of Beman's letters, and discovered that a second school was far from the only choice. He expressed a hope that the CSC would consider the report well, "for we need a fresh approach to the solution. The issue is a community problem and the solution must serve the needs of the entire community."

Beman's letters also elicited a public denial by Board President Long that the Board and administration were committed to any one solution. The preface to the Cornog-Brown Report, Long declared, made it clear that the pro and con arguments of each of the five alternatives were intended only to "stimulate thinking." He also rejected Beman's contention that the members of the CSC had been selected to weight the recommendations in favor of preconceived Board plans. Rather, said Long, they were chosen "as representing the total New Trier Township Community."[23]

[23] *Wilmette Life*, September 21, 1961.

The exchange was not over, however. Beman replied a week later:

> The Board has just one commitment: finding an alternative to the last proposal. It was thus committed by the voters last Spring.
>
> Obviously Superintendent Cornog's bulletin could not cover every argument, every alternative. But it does cover basic issues. Most who carefully study it wonder how the last proposal ever reached the voters. Are we now faced with a repudiation of this bulletin . . . ?
>
> At first glance, Mr. Long's remarks about the objectivity of the citizens' committee are reassuring. However school publicity in the July 13th issue of this newspaper says: "Dr. Cornog will provide the committee with educational evaluation of their plans." But the September 15th *New Trier News* quotes him as saying: "The only way to preserve New Trier is to divide it."
>
> What use is there in a jury studying possible verdicts when the judge announces flatly and publicly that only one verdict is acceptable?
>
> I have talked with too many educators, including members of the New Trier faculty, . . . to accept any statement that one solution is the only solution, particularly when, by its very nature that solution is derisive and inflammatory.
>
> The School Board is apparently determined to resubmit the same old proposition, hoping to increase its share of the vote from 44 per cent to 51 per cent. Perhaps it is only human nature to avoid admitting a mistake. But wouldn't it be better all around if an alternative were developed which gave everyone equal treatment? Then we could strive not for a 51 per cent plurality but for 100 per cent.[24]

Beman's description of the Northfield proposal as "derisive and inflammatory" drew a quick reply from a New Trier faculty member, who felt that referendum opponents took a position "cloaked in innuendo." He questioned Beman's citation of anonymous educators who opposed the second school proposal on undisclosed grounds. Arguing for a second high

[24] *Wilmette Life*, September 28, 1961.

school, he concluded: "In ten years, when loyalties are established and traditions cemented, when a first class faculty is teaching a first class student body in a first rate plant, bitter feelings will be forgotten and fallacious notions about unequal treatment will be forgotten."[25]

This letter caused quite a stir throughout the community for three reasons: (a) the writer's father was a member of the Citizens' Study Committee, and many thought the letter had been written by the father; (b) a letter from Superintendent Cornog appeared in the same issue, immediately following it, declaring that "advocacy by anyone associated with New Trier is quite out of order"; and (c) it supported the notion that a second school would not be equal to the old one immediately. A new series of letters followed making all of these points.

By the end of October, 1961, the Real Estate Research Corporation had concluded its population study and submitted a detailed report to the Citizens' Study Committee. The highlights were reported in the Hollister papers on November 2. In general, the RERC figures confirmed those of the 1960 Brown Report for the 1960–70 decade.[26] But whereas Brown had projected a peak of 5,560 in 1971, to be followed by a "normal saturation level" of 5,278 about 1975, the RERC report predicted gradual increases all during the 1970–80 decade and estimated New Trier enrollment at 6,388 by 1980.[27]

Equipped with the new population projections of the RERC, which it considered reliable, the Citizens' Study Committee was able to complete its study and submit its report within three weeks. Obviously alarmed by the specter

[25] *Wilmette Life*, October 5, 1961.
[26] Wesley Brown, "A Prediction of Maximum Enrollment After Building Saturation for New Trier Township High School District" (revised; 19 pp., mimeo.; New Trier Township High School, July 14, 1961).
[27] Real Estate Research Corporation, *High School Enrollment Projections for New Trier High School* (28 pp.; prepared for the New Trier Board of Education, Oct., 1961).

of a 6,300-student high school, the CSC "with unanimity and without reservation" recommended a second four-year high school to be built for 2,500 students. For all intents and purposes, this recommendation signaled the end of the one-site-versus-two controversy. Thereafter, the community seemed to accept the fact that a second four-year school was necessary.

The committee's choice of a site for the second school, however, was not so readily accepted. The site subcommittee had thoroughly considered fourteen sites, of which it was determined only six were adequate (employing criteria of location, cost, availability, accessibility). Of these six—two in Winnetka, two in Wilmette, the Northfield site previously rejected, and the area adjacent to the existing New Trier High School campus on its north and west—the subcommittee unanimously recommended and the full committee approved a forty-acre site on the southwest corner of Hibbard and Willow roads in Winnetka. It was described as the "best" and "least expensive" site in the District. New Trier already owned ten of the forty acres as a result of the 1959 negotiations with Winnetka for athletic fields. Twenty acres belonged to the village of Winnetka and the remaining ten were owned by the Cook County Forest Preserve District. The Northfield site was the Committee's fourth choice, but it ranked second in terms of availability because it was virtually unimproved.

A third recommendation of the CSC concerned attendance-area districting. The School Board had suggested this item for inclusion on the committee's agenda, hoping that such a representative group could arrive at a palatable solution to this exceedingly delicate problem in community relations. The CSC recommendation, based on the Hibbard-Willow site, would have retained in the district to be served by the old school Kenilworth, Wilmette, most of the Avoca elementary district (largely unincorporated, but including small sections of Glenview and Wilmette), and a strip of Winnetka along Lake Michigan. Students from Glencoe, Sunset Ridge (Northfield), the remainder of Winnetka, and part of Avoca would attend the new school (see Figure 3). It was thought that this apportionment would remove the objections to the lines previously proposed by the Board.

A few days after the contents of the CSC report were made public, the School Board met with the Winnetka village council and village manager, the CSC, and the platform committee of the 1962 Winnetka Caucus, which would be meeting in six weeks. This meeting provided the first hints that perhaps Winnetka would not agree to sell its land to the school. Council President Vernon Welsh stated that Winnetka did not want to obstruct a new high school. "We are sensitive about the problem of educating the young. We have a proud record and don't want to impair it. But the Citizens' Study Committee has handed us a very knotty problem."

Ostensibly, the "knotty problem" involved four elements:

(a) Part of the land was being used for dry dumping. Although the Forest Preserve District had agreed to allow Winnetka to dump on its land farther west, Winnetka officials feared that this would raise dumping costs 15 to 20 per cent.
(b) The village had planned a new generating plant for that site. Building a high school there would further increase the load on the present plant.
(c) Police costs would be increased.
(d) Access roads would have to be widened, at considerable cost to the village.

Following the joint meeting, support for the proposed plan came from the Winnetka Caucus platform committee,

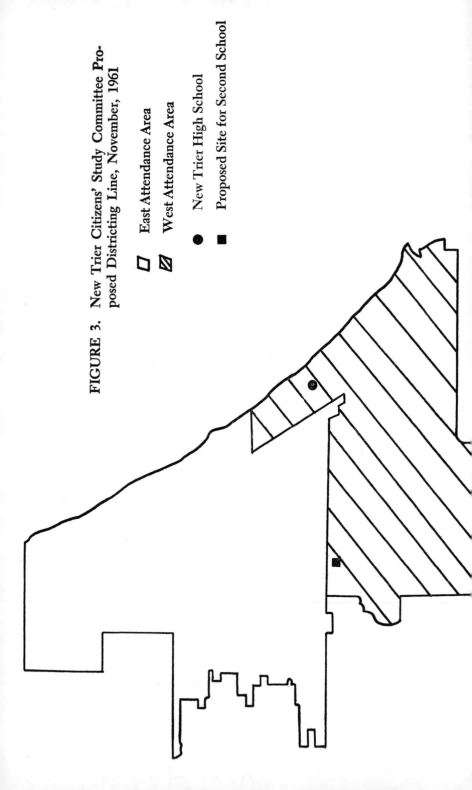

FIGURE 3. New Trier Citizens' Study Committee Proposed Districting Line, November, 1961

☐ East Attendance Area

▨ West Attendance Area

● New Trier High School

■ Proposed Site for Second School

which promptly endorsed the CSC program by a 28–10 vote. The Hollister editorial of December 14 called it a "wise" and "practical" solution to the problem. In the same issue, the results of a telephone survey conducted by the paper were revealed: 55 per cent of those questioned favored a second four-year school, 23 per cent opposed it, and 22 per cent had no opinion. The Board of Education passed a resolution endorsing the committee's recommendation for establishing a second four-year school, and stated its interest in the Winnetka site "if it is available in full and promptly."

The response in Winnetka was mixed. The CSC plan was endorsed by the Winnetka board of education, which felt that Winnetka was "the strategic community in the Township in realization of the important measures that must be taken if our public schools are to remain sound."

On the other hand, there was the chauvinistic attitude expressed by one Winnetkan in a letter to the "Public Forum":

> After providing a home for the Township's High School for better than half a century, it seems less than fair for Winnetka to bear the burden of the proposed New Trier West as well.
>
> It is time for Winnetka residents to stop letting the rest of the Township push us around. Northfielders who have already crowded us off our beaches, don't want the new high school in their village—for reasons not completely honorable.
>
> Now Wilmette is being given New Trier East as a gift. Will Glencoe come forward with its demands next?[28]

Another letter writer felt that Winnetka had given freely enough of its land in the past and opposed the proposal: "The Willow-Hibbard site is good for the Township but bad for Winnetka." This Winnetkan argued that the village needed the land for present and future projects, and that the area

[28] *Wilmette Life*, December 28, 1961.

served as a floodgate to prevent over-population of the village. "It would be unique, indeed preposterous, if Winnetka had to shoulder the responsibilities of a second high school when Wilmette, with over twice the population and still growing has no public high school at all. Winnetka had foresight when the other towns were myopic; let's keep our open land."[29]

On January 8, the Board received and studied an architectural firm's favorable report on the feasibility of the Willow-Hibbard site for a high school. By a four-to-two vote, a resolution was adopted supporting continued negotiations with the village of Winnetka for acquisition of the Willow-Hibbard site.

The turning point in the Board's negotiations with the reluctant village council came on January 23 at the Winnetka annual town meeting (Caucus). The platform committee's qualified endorsement of the Willow-Hibbard site attracted the largest crowd ever assembled for a town meeting in Winnetka. Following presentations in support of the proposal by representatives of the CSC and the New Trier Board of Education (both Winnetkans) and an explanation of its drawbacks by Council President Welsh, the meeting voted to reject the platform plank advocating a second school on the Willow-Hibbard site. In its stead, a plank was adopted which required that, when and if the village trustees decide "to dispose of Village property for this purpose, then their decision shall be submitted to the voters in a legal referendum."

The council president told the meeting that the trustees had not had time for a thorough study to determine if the village could afford to sell land it had planned to use for expanded and improved services. Any decision would have to be preceded by a complete study using professional help. The council, remembering the rejection of a utility-sale referendum in 1957, and the fact that eighty residents had attended a

[29] *Ibid.*

recent council meeting to protest the sale of the site to New Trier, was in no hurry to make a decision.[30]

A special meeting of the Board of Education was held on Sunday, January 28, to review the site situation in the light of the Winnetka Caucus referendum plank and the failure of the Winnetka village council to make a decision. The Board was afraid that further delay would make it impossible to complete the new school by September, 1964, forcing the student body to go on double shifts. The Board accordingly decided to send a letter to the Winnetka council requesting that it reach a decision regarding the sale of the Willow-Hibbard site "as promptly as possible and in any event not later than the middle of February." It was further requested that if the decision were favorable, the referendum required by the town meeting be held not later than mid-April.

This letter was followed up by a meeting between Welsh and two Board members. The village council still wanted an outside, professional study of village needs before it would commit itself.

At its next meeting (February 5), the School Board decided to advise the Winnetka trustees that it favored action *without* additional study, since this study would take a minimum of sixty days, but if it was required the high school would have it done by the Real Estate Research Corporation. At the council meeting three days later, the trustees decided once again that a professional study of village needs would have to precede any decision to sell public land to the school. The council estimated that the study would take sixty to ninety days, after which that body would make its decision. If this was favorable, six more weeks would be required for a village-wide referendum on the question.

[30] For a detailed analysis of the way in which the Winnetka village council decision-making process operates, see James B. Holderman, *Decision-Making and Community Leadership in the Village of Winnetka, Illinois* (unpublished Ph.D. dissertation, Northwestern University, 1962).

Charles Kaufman, a Winnetkan representing the School Board at the council meeting, said that, notwithstanding the delay, "we still want to negotiate for the site. We will gladly join in a professional study of Village land needs and possible alternative sites for a second school." The real question, he maintained was whether Winnetka so needed the property that it *must not* sell it to the high school. Welsh replied that the study would have to be made first. "A referendum held today without additional information about our needs and the feasibility of selecting other sites for the school, would be turned down."[31]

The village of Winnetka proceeded to talk with the Real Estate Research Corporation concerning a land-need study. On February 17, the Board received a letter from Welsh stating that the RERC had advised the council against making such a study. Two paragraphs from the RERC letter to Welsh were quoted:

> The inevitable conclusion of the study of the Willow-Hibbard site as it would affect Winnetka would be that the Village will need an increasing amount of land in the future and that it would be desirable to retain this parcel. This is not to say that this need would be stronger than that of the second high school; if this were the *only* site I'm sure that the latter would prevail. Thus the only way that such a need for the Village can be considered in its proper perspective is to evaluate it as one of many factors affecting the selection of a preferred site and to include need for land for other public purposes as one of the significant criteria in a site selection study.
>
> In view of the above it is our recommendation that the New Trier Board of Education take action to secure a detailed professional site selection study.

Welsh indicated that he, the council, and the village manager agreed with the RERC recommendation.

Apprised of this development, the Board proceeded to

31 *Wilmette Life*, February 8, 1962.

reconsider the entire land-acquisition problem. September, 1964, two and a half years away, was the target date for a completed second school. It was estimated that four to six months would elapse even before a referendum could be held in Winnetka on the land sale. Were the referendum defeated, that time would have been lost and there would be no site. More and more the Board members were becoming convinced that Winnetkans did not want to give up their land but that, because an educational issue was involved, they found it difficult to come right out and say "no."

The alternatives to Willow-Hibbard were re-evaluated. Although ranked fourth in terms of desirability by the CSC, the previously rejected Northfield site ranked second in availability. Since the same Board had considered this the "best available" site less than a year ago, there was strong sentiment that this site should again be sought, although Scott, Foresman and Company now owned (but had not yet developed) twenty-five of the forty-five acres. Furthermore, in Northfield, the Board could use its condemnation powers, if necessary; this strategy was not available in its pursuit of the Willow-Hibbard area which was owned by governmental units.

The other sites listed by the CSC as "suitable" were also briefly reconsidered. The thirty-five acres owned by the Forest Preserve District at Winnetka and Hibbard roads (in Winnetka) was quickly dismissed, since the District had made it clear that its general policy was to retain *all* its property. The so-called Mallenckrodt property in Wilmette was owned and used by the Sisters of Christian Charity, had a cemetery on it, was developed, and, according to the Mother Superior, was not for sale. A fourth possibility was the 107-acre Northwestern University–owned golf course, but the Board rejected this because of its relatively poor location in the extreme southwest corner of the District.

The Board had not given up hope completely on the Willow-Hibbard site. It decided to inform the Winnetka council that it saw no reason to have the RERC restudy the available school sites in the District, since the Board and the CSC had thoroughly explored them over the past two years. Furthermore, while the Board considered the Willow-Hibbard site the most desirable from the standpoint of the educational needs of the township, the Northfield site was "available and suitable" although not as "attractive" as the one in Winnetka.

It was not entirely unexpected, then, that the Winnetka village council unanimously refused to sell its property to the Board without a "professional study of possible school sites." One trustee summed up the council's position in these words:

> Since the High School Board isn't willing to conduct a professional site study, I don't feel we should sell the land. We know this land will be used if we keep it and I'm not prepared to sacrifice it without a professional recommendation to that effect.[32]

Deprived of its first choice by the Winnetka council, the School Board quickly turned to the alternatives. The Northfield site appeared to be the sentimental favorite among the members, and the probability of its being selected was enhanced by the "not for sale" declarations issued by other site owners following the Winnetka vote. The Sisters of Christian Charity reiterated that they had "no intention whatsoever" of disposing of the Mallenckrodt property. Northwestern University released a statement indicating its intentions of using the Wilmette golf course for a research park.

Although revised School Board intentions were not announced publicly until April 1, it became clear much earlier that the Board had decided to go after the Northfield site again. Since February 7, before the Winnetka council vote, Board members had been in communication with Northfield village officials, and had met with the representatives of Scott,

[32] *Wilmette Life*, February 22, 1962.

Foresman to inform them of the possibility of another referendum for that site. After Winnetka rejected the sale of the Willow-Hibbard site, the Board pursued the Northfield site more aggressively, although rezoning had doubled the estimated cost per acre since the 1961 referendum.

Dismayed over what was happening, executives of the three firms concerned with the Northfield site—Chapman of Scott, Foresman, Leander of Mystic Tape, and Stepan of Stepan Chemical—took steps to save their land from condemnation. They had heard through the North Shore "grapevine" (fifteen Northwestern University trustees live on the North Shore) that Northwestern would consider selling its golf course to raise money for a program of campus expansion into Lake Michigan. They went to Northwestern business manager William Kerr, and discussed the possibility of their buying all 107 acres at the university's asking price of $28,500 per acre ($3,000,000) and reselling it to New Trier and the Wilmette park board at cost. Approached by Chapman concerning such a "deal," the School Board declined, citing the poor location and the inaccessibility of the plot. The Board said that its information was that the university land was not for sale, but "even if it were available, we would still prefer the Happ-Winnetka [Northfield] location."[33]

J. Stanley Blum (Glenview), site chairman of the defunct CSC, was still convinced that either the Northwestern golf course in Wilmette or the "ideal" site owned by the Forest Preserve District in Winnetka was superior to the Northfield site which the School Board seemed determined to get. With the assistance of Michael Greenebaum (Glencoe), also a member of the CSC, and a power in Cook County Democratic politics, Blum was able to arrange possible land-exchanges with the superintendent of the Forest Preserve District and with Northwestern University. His notion was for the high school to buy the 380-acre Edison Dick estate in the

[33] *Wilmette Life*, April 5, 1962.

western part of Cook County for $2,000 per acre (this price was firm) and exchange it with either the Forest Preserve or Northwestern for one of the other sites. The superintendent of the Forest Preserve District was sure the district commissioners would approve of the idea, since they would be getting 300 acres for 35, but he pointed out that the exchange would have to be approved by an act of the Illinois legislature, which was not scheduled to convene until January, 1962. The university also indicated a willingness to exchange, because the 107 acres in Wilmette was deemed too small for an adequate research park. The Board of Education declined to participate in either arrangement.

In a speech to the Wilmette PTA a few days later, Blum revealed the nature of these alternatives. He had decided that the Board simply was not interested in any site but Northfield, and he felt that the public should know the "truth" about the other alternatives. Greenebaum was asked by the Board to write a letter to the "Public Forum" repudiating Blum and denying the "deals," but he refused.

Despite the fact that three new Board members, who would be bound by the decision, were to be elected in April, on March 31, 1962, the "old" Board voted unanimously to acquire the Northfield site, and it set June 9 as the referendum date.[34] A few weeks later the bond issue was set at $1,825,000, double the 1961 estimated cost.

With the decision made, the Board's next step was to determine how best to "sell" the decision to the community. Remembering that the 1961 referendum defeat was attributed to poor salesmanship, the trustees were determined not to make the same mistakes twice. The Board appointed a public relations subcommittee, which in turn recommended that a

[34] Four uncontested candidates were to be elected, but one (Charles Sprowl, Glencoe) was an incumbent. Originally only three vacancies would have occurred in 1962, but Marshall Long, Board president, resigned "for business reasons."

small volunteer group of professional public relations executives residing in the community be asked to serve as a consulting committee. Its function would be

> to recommend the type and outline the organization of a campaign . . . with recommendations for (a) a schedule of mailings, (b) local press coverage, (c) use of other news media, (d) type and number of public meetings, (e) type and organization of printed information, and (f) organization and operation of an implementing or working committee.[35]

The president of a large Chicago advertising agency (a Winnetkan) was asked to chair this group. Within ten days he had a six-man group, named the New Trier Information Committee, at work, and had assigned a liaison man to work half time with Superintendent Cornog's administrative assistant.

The major difference between the 1961 and 1962 campaigns for the Northfield site was one of strategy. One Board member summarized the approach in the first referendum in this way:

> We went into the first referendum feeling we were the chosen representatives of the people; we agonized over the decision we had made and felt that all we had to do was explain the decision to them and have it accepted. The strategy was to put the members of the Board and administration on a platform at a series of meetings and have them present the proposal; this was bad procedure because we couldn't adequately handle the opponents who attended every meeting and asked the same damaging questions. They used the "big lie" technique at these meetings—blew up the cost figures and the "Jewish problem."[36]

Cornog's administrative assistant saw the difference between the first and second campaigns in terms of the Board's and the superintendent's role:

[35] Minutes, New Trier Board of Education meeting, March 12, 1962.
[36] Interview with Loring Farwell (Northfield), November 30, 1962.

In the first referendum we depended on a series of public meetings. We invited elementary schools to organize resident meetings, with speeches given by Board members and administrative personnel. This gave the opponents a chance to be vocal, and they went from one meeting to another. We feel we influenced very few votes using this method.

The second time, the Board felt Cornog should concern himself primarily with running the school, but he was kept fully informed by the Board, the Information Committee, and myself. I represented the administration on the committee. All Cornog's statements were co-ordinated through the committee. Lloyd Hollister [president of Hollister Press] was contacted and agreed to support the Committee's public relations activities. He had a reporter at every meeting and gave us good coverage. We relied on two direct mailings to all residents, six full-page ads in the Hollister papers, and press coverage of the Board meetings. The one public dinner at which the Board appeared reinforced our notions regarding the opportunity this gives the opposition to be vocal.[37]

In addition to the Information Committee, which was primarily an advisory group, a working committee known as the Committee for Two New Triers was formed. It was composed of over one thousand residents of the district who volunteered as block workers in response to a letter sent by the Information Committee to every household. A general chairman was named, and co-chairmen were appointed in each village. In the weeks prior to the June 9 referendum, the block workers visited every household in the District at least once, urging residents to support the referendum.

A third arm of the public relations program was the cause of some complaints. In mid-May, the students at the high school organized a Student Action Committee to promote passage of the referendum. Assemblies were held in the school at which Board members spoke. When petitions were circulated in the school to enlist volunteers to conduct a house-to-house canvass of the District, 71 per cent of the student

---

[37] Interview with Robert Harper, July 19, 1962.

body responded. The student group even ran a few ads in the Hollister papers emphasizing the overcrowded conditions at the school and urging support of the referendum.

The complaints stemmed from citizens who felt the students were being manipulated and coerced by the Board and the public relations people:

> The students were extremely eager to help; but this was a delicate situation. In the last few weeks of the campaign we received many complaints from irate parents saying that their child was being "coerced." The chairman of the Young Republicans in Winnetka felt that if the kids were "used" in this way, she should be able to open a chapter at the school. Cornog, of course, said "no." The Information Committee counseled the student group *when they requested it.* For example, we told them not to run two additional ads in the last week although they had the money; we didn't want them too involved in this thing. The students got their funds from the Committee for Two New Triers, donations from citizens, and by passing the hat.[38]

The well-organized and well-administered public relations program was no doubt the most significant difference in the second referendum as compared with the first. But the probability of success was also increased by a number of other factors. First among these was the Board's revised approach to the delicate problem of redistricting. Rather than risk antagonizing one section of the township by specifying attendance areas in advance, the Board announced, on April 30, that it considered it "premature" to draw lines before the new school was ready for occupancy. At the same time it went a long way toward appeasing the Northfield and west Wilmette voters by adding that it recognized "the desirability of having students from the major villages in both schools."

A second factor enhancing the chances of the proposal

[38] Interview with Everett Tretbar, public relations advisor to New Trier High School, August 29, 1962.

was the Board's decision in mid-April to buy six mobile classrooms to accommodate the expected classroom overflow in the fall of 1962. The publicity given to this decision, complete with pictures of the mobile classrooms in the Hollister papers, helped to impress upon the community the seriousness of the situation faced by the District. One of the wealthiest communities in America was not ready or willing to accept this kind of solution to the problem of inadequate school facilities.

Third, there was overwhelming public support of the referendum by individuals and groups throughout the District. In addition to the citizens who actively participated as block workers for the Committee for Two New Triers, and the New Trier Student Action Committee, the referendum gained the support of the League of Women Voters in the District, representing over a thousand women; 90 per cent of the combined membership voted to support the Board's proposition. Four of the six elementary school boards in the District publicly avowed their endorsement, as did the parent-teachers' associations in these districts. The influential New Trier Parents' Association lent its support of the referendum and ran several full-page ads to make its position known. A group calling itself the "Northfield Residents for a New Trier Bond Issue" also announced its support in a full-page ad, as did several other miscellaneous groups. Numerous individuals pleaded the Board's case in the "Public Forum," and numbers of citizens contributed money and lent their names to multi-page ads to express their opinion and to try to influence the opinions of others.

Although a "bandwagon" effect was created by the public relations campaign and by the growing desire within the community to avoid further delay in the construction of new facilities, the Board's 1962 proposal did not go uncontested. There were, however, significant differences between the kinds of opposition faced by the first and by the second referenda.

In the first place, the strategy employed by the School Board in the 1962 referendum campaign—detailed direct mailings, numerous ads, and a vigorous people-to-people program—forced the opponents to play by Board rules, a procedure for which they had neither organization nor resources. In 1962 the opponents were unable simply to follow the Board from meeting to meeting and ask the same embarrassing and damaging questions, although in 1961 this strategy had influenced those in attendance and had gotten the opponents good press coverage gratis. In 1962, they were forced to fight a battle of newspaper ads, which not only were expensive but required them to identify themselves as adversaries; few were willing to pay the cost in money or in possible public disapproval.

A second difference was in the nature of the objections to the Board's program. In 1961, opposition came from a variety of sources. Some citizens were upset by the high cost of expansion; others were opposed to dividing the student body; and still others, even if they accepted the concept of a second four-year high school, objected to the site selected. In 1962, cost became a minor issue, even though the price had doubled, and the need for a second four-year school was generally accepted by the community following the Real Estate Research Corporation's prediction of a 6,300-student enrollment. The 1962 opposition developed around objections to the Board's decision to go after the Northfield site again. But instead of merely objecting, as was the case in 1961, the 1962 opponents exerted considerable effort and spent much time assembling facts and figures to disparage the Northfield site and to make a case for their particular choice of a site.

The third difference lay in the identity of the adversaries. The identifiable, i.e., vocal, opponents to the Board's 1961 proposal were replaced by an entirely new group in 1962. Those who had voiced disapproval of the 1961 referendum, including outspoken Northfielder Jeremy Beman, had been either convinced or appeased by the Board in 1962.[39] Although fewer in number, the 1962 opponents were no more organized as a group; each pursued his or her own alternative to the Board's choice, motivated by a variety of reasons.

Five individuals constituted the School Board's serious opposition in 1962. Two of them—Mrs. Frances Hall (Winnetka) and Roy Pavlik (Kenilworth)—operated independently, while the other three—Ray Fowler (Winnetka), Robert Sale (Wilmette), and Lee Ahlswede (Northfield)—formed a loose coalition after it was discovered they were all interested in the same thing, although for very different reasons.

Mrs. Hall, although opposed to the 1961 referendum, had not become involved in the activities of the opponents to that measure. It was not until January, 1962, when she heard the rumor that the Northwestern University golf course might be available, that she became active. She said she felt that it was the only site large enough (fifty-five acres was her minimum); it was also "pretty," had a good location, and could be reached by good access roads. In addition, she argued, Northfield had by then rezoned the site in that village, increasing the cost to $40,000 per acre, whereas the Northwestern University site was available for $27,500 per acre. Furthermore, if the Northfield site were used, it would cost the township $289,000 annually in taxes (though one-half of all taxes went to New Trier High School). The Northwestern property was already tax-exempt.

> I called three Northwestern trustees who live on the North Shore, although I didn't know them, and they substantiated my belief that the golf course was available *if the*

[39] Beman, who led the Northfield objectors in the first referendum, and who threatened to do so again when the Board decided to try for the Northfield site in 1962, threw his support behind the Board when it assured him that districting would be in accordance with the so-called "major villages" plan; i.e., the student population of Wilmette, Winnetka, and Glencoe would be divided between the two schools.

*School Board asked for it.* I then sent a letter to the Board on February 26 suggesting that they pursue this. This was after Winnetka turned them down and before they decided to try for Northfield again. Assistant Superintendent Brown told me that he had spoken with [Northwestern business manager William] Kerr and was told that this was true—the golf course was available for $27,500 per acre. This information was reported to the Board meeting that evening but it got not a single word in the Hollister press.[40]

By attending every Board meeting, Mrs. Hall continued to put the Northwestern University site alternative before the Board at every opportunity, but with no results. On April 4, after rejecting an offer by the Northfield industrialist group to buy and resell to the School Board part of the Northwestern University site, the Board *requested* and received a letter from Northwestern University President Roscoe Miller stating, in part, that "so far as the University is concerned [the golf course] cannot be regarded as available." Mrs. Hall discounted this, because she subsequently learned that Miller had agreed to a Cornog-Long request not to make the land "available" until after the referendum so as not to embarrass the Board, which did not like the site.

On June 4, only days before the referendum election, Mrs. Hall called President Miller and demanded to know how he could say the land was not available when his business manager and at least three Northwestern University trustees said it was. Miller referred her to the influential chairman of the trustees' Committee on Property, Foster McGaw. Mrs. Hall called and was told that McGaw had been out of the country for the past six months, a fact she was sure Miller knew. But McGaw returned on June 6 and called Mrs. Hall. He confirmed the availability of the site but reiterated that the School Board would have to ask for it before the university board of trustees' meeting scheduled for June 11 (two days *after* the referendum).

[40] Interview with Frances Hall, October 30, 1962.

I stayed up all that night typing letters to the Chicago newspapers regarding the change of events, but at 7:45 the next morning, McGaw called back and said that he had reconsidered and thought he had better back out, since it was so close to the referendum date. We had been double-crossed again.

I had [Chicago CBS newscaster] Fahey Flynn out here to my home on the morning of the 8th to tape an interview for his 6 P.M. and 10 P.M. news programs regarding the Northwestern University site availability, but I refused to let him use it unless it was cleared with a Northwestern trustee. It wasn't cleared in time, and on Saturday we were beaten.[41]

Mrs. Hall worked hard to promote her idea for the Northwestern University site, but Roy Pavlik of Kenilworth worked even harder for his plan. Convinced that New Trier High School boards "have performed very poorly in the matter of acquiring land for future expansion," and that "taxes were running out of hand," Pavlik spent $1,200 of his own funds and countless hours in a futile attempt to convince the Board and the community that the answer to the site problem was for the Cook County Forest Preserve District to "donate" to the high school a forty-five acre tract at Winnetka and Hibbard roads in Winnetka. He argued, in three two-page ads in the Hollister papers, at Board meetings, and in letters to the "Public Forum," (a) that the Forest Preserve owned too much (12 per cent) of the land in the New Trier District; (b) that use of privately owned land such as the Northfield site would cost the taxpayers $2,000,000 plus the loss of $250,000 in taxes every year; (c) that it did *not* take an act of the Illinois legislature, contrary to the School Board's contention, for the Forest Preserve District to give away land outright, only a two-thirds vote of the district commissioners; (d) that there was precedent for such a donation by the district; and (e) that the tract desired was "out of line" with

[41] *Ibid.*

the rest of the preserve land, was unused, and could never be used in conjunction with the other parts.

Pavlik's efforts elicited little visible support. One "Public Forum" letter from Wilmette agreed that the site was "ideal," making "all the other possible sites for a second New Trier High School seem very inadequate by comparison . . . even if we have to purchase [it]." Pavlik's only other support came in the form of two anonymous offers of financial support totaling $1,100, to send a mailing to every household in the district just before the referendum. He declined, because he felt he was beaten by that time.

Pavlik's ads, however, did succeed in arousing the ire of the superintendent of the Forest Preserve District and of one annoyed "Public Forum" contributor who felt that Pavlik was misleading the community:

> Roy Pavlik's demands for the forest preserve to give land to New Trier High School are having the same obstructionist effects that led to the defeat of the previous referendum.
>
> His ads are misleading and are a disservice to our community. They mislead because they suggest that there is recent precedence of land being given to schools, when the fact is that there has been no land so given up for the past twenty years.
>
> Second, they suggest that inadequate overtures have been made to the forest preserve, when the fact is that repeated requests have been made, and the forest preserve has just as repeatedly declared that their land is unavailable.
>
> Third, they state that in "a dire emergency" the forest preserve can be made to give New Trier land, when the fact is that though we urgently need land for a new school, such land is available and we are having a referendum next month to buy it.
>
> Among the most attractive features of our suburbs are the green parks, fields, and forest that prevent our being built up "wall-to-wall." These preserves provide recreational havens for ourselves and for the larger community that includes New Trier Township.

> Any inroads into this park system are in themselves, and in the precedents they set, detrimental to the lovely communities we all have chosen to make our homes in.
>
> These ads create dissension and doubt when we need unity in purpose to obtain the available site that can and should be approved now, rather than allow ourselves to be dragged into further bickering and postponement.[42]

In mid-May, Forest Preserve Superintendent Charles Sauers attempted to refute Pavlik's claim that the district could "give" land to New Trier High School.[43] He cited no statutes, but nonetheless his statement left the impression that it was impossible for the Forest Preserve District to give land away to anyone. He said that the precedent Pavlik referred to in his ads concerned four cases in the 1920's and one in 1942 in which the Forest Preserve did transfer land to school districts, but added:

> It was apparent such allocations were wrong and should cease. No departure from our holding policy has been made since 1942 . . . it would be strange indeed if the policy were to be broken for the wealthiest suburban high school district in the county.
>
> [Glencoe, Winnetka, and Wilmette] are buffered and protected on their western boundaries by Forest Preserve lands with seventy-five per cent of the funds for them coming from Chicago taxpayers. These meadows, forests, and lagoons—twelve per cent of the New Trier area—are the very thing cities and villages throughout the United States are trying to obtain and which city planners consider ideal. They give beauty, spaciousness and dignity to the New Trier scene. . . . It is the expressed and formally stated intention of the Forest Preserve Commissioners to hold these lands which are the property of more than five million persons.

And one of the district commissioners stated:

> All the people in Cook County contributed to the purchase of this land in New Trier Township. It never was owned just by New Trier residents. . . . For more than

[42] *Wilmette Life,* May 17, 1962.
[43] *Ibid.*

twenty years not one foot of forest preserve land has been released. If we gave away this parcel, we would open the door to giving away the rest of the forest preserves to other school districts.

Neither the superintendent nor the commissioner once said that they *could not* surrender the tract; less than two months before, they had seriously considered the deal offered by Blum and Greenebaum for the same tract. It was clear, however, that they *would not* give it away; and, since the Forest Preserve District was a public body, the School District could not condemn the land. Pavlik's cause was lost.

The third pocket of active resistance encountered by the School Board came to be known as the "Committee for Two New Triers on a Wilmette Site" (CTNTWS). Although it organised only in mid-May, this group managed to solicit ten-dollar contributions from over sixty people, run a two-page ad (which Board members had privately asked them to withdraw), and distribute 5,000 reprints of the ad before the referendum. But, as the chairman later admitted: "We just weren't organized to handle an opposition to the Board."

The CTNTWS came into being rather fortuitously. Robert Sale of Wilmette, a surveyor–civil engineer who had done work for New Trier on possible sites for the second school, became interested in having it located in Wilmette. He felt that the high school had to compromise on its curriculum to meet vast curriculum differences among the elementary districts of the township; his idea was to put all the Wilmette districts into one high school *located in Wilmette*. On several occasions after Winnetka's refusal to sell, Sale offered what he considered to be constructive assistance to the Board regarding possible Wilmette sites. "They listened awhile and then ignored me."

But on May 17, Ray Fowler of Winnetka wrote a letter to the "Public Forum" explaining why he would vote "no" on the upcoming referendum.

Wilmette is one of the few municipalities of its size in the country that does not provide a public high school site. It accounts for about forty per cent of New Trier's students. This is approximately equal to the number of students that make the second school mandatory.

Since Wilmette is by far the largest suburb concerned, it is only proper that the School Board offer Wilmette this option: "You pick a site in your community or we will."

When Sale saw Fowler's letter, he realized that others also favored placing the second high school in Wilmette, although for different reasons (Sale was convinced that Winnetkans wanted to get rid of the "newcomers" in west Wilmette). He called Fowler, explained his position, and they agreed to work together. They contacted Lee Ahlswede, a Northfielder who had supported Jeremy Beman's opposition to the 1961 referendum, and who felt that the School Board was "morally wrong" in trying to promote the idea of a Northfield site once again in 1962. His opposition to date had consisted of several letters to the "Public Forum," in which he stressed the wisdom of locating the school in the "area [which has] the most rapidly expanding population . . . delivering about forty-five per cent of the New Trier enrollment, and [which] has further expansion and high-rise apartments on the way," i.e., Wilmette.

Sale, Fowler, and Ahlswede met at Fowler's home four times in the two or three weeks before the referendum. Fowler became chairman of the group, and the three men worked out a program to publicize their joint opinion about the desirability of a Wilmette site. Mrs. Hall was invited, and met once with the others, but she was interested only in the Northwestern University golf course, and worked alone most of the time. The members of the CTNTWS were more flexible; they would accept almost any Wilmette site.

In fact, they worked actively for three of them—the thirty-acre Mallenckrodt property in central Wilmette, a twenty-nine-acre farm in south Wilmette, and the Northwestern University site—all previously considered by the Citizens' Study Committee in the fall of 1961. In spite of the group's enthusiasm, the Board paid little attention. But on June 1, just eight days before the referendum, Fowler learned from a Northwestern University trustee, as had Mrs. Hall and the Northfield industrialists before him, that the golf course was available to the School Board. Through a series of phone calls, Fowler, Sale, and Ahlswede were directed to a "source" who would authoritatively verify the availability of the golf course to the Board. They then met with this man who told them that, in a conference with President Miller, he had been "strongly urged" not to become involved in the situation; he suggested that they might talk with business manager William Kerr. Kerr was shown a statement, originally prepared by the CTNTWS for the "source," in which the university's position regarding the site was concisely outlined. Kerr agreed that the document stated the situation clearly and signed it on June 3. The members of the CTNTWS felt that they had an eleventh-hour victory in sight; they planned to exploit the signed document to the embarrassment of the School Board. But later that evening, Kerr called Fowler and said that, in a conference he had had with President Miller, it was decided that the university did not want to risk possible future condemnation of the golf course by publicizing its availability.[44] Kerr requested that his name be withdrawn from

[44] In an interview with William Kerr (November 16, 1962), he answered questions concerning Northwestern University's position as follows:
    Q. What was the university's role in the New Trier conflict?
    A. It all ties in with the lake-front project. In January, 1962, we had an anonymous gift of $2,500,000 for the lake project from a trustee who prefers to remain unknown. We knew the project would cost about $6,500,000, so we had to raise $4,000,000. We took a long look at the property we owned which we might sell and soon decided to sell one piece in Chicago that we were sure we would never use; this would help "create land" up here. Board of trustees by-laws stipulate that no land can be *sold* without authority of the full board. The board did adopt a general policy that they would approve the sale of "any land which could not and would never be used for campus

the statement. Fowler complied but did not return the document.

The members of the CTNTWS were disappointed by what they considered to be a "double-cross." They were sure that School Board member Allen Stults (Wilmette) had "gotten to" President Miller, and that he in turn had told Kerr to stay out of the controversy. Nonetheless, they proceeded to submit a two-page ad for the June 7 issue of the

expansion" in order to raise money for the lake project; this policy included the golf course, but it was not specifically mentioned.

In line with this policy, the golf course was appraised in April, 1962, at approximately $28,000 an acre for the 107 acres, or $2,900,-000 for the site. This land was not for sale to private developers for single-family tract housing, although I get about fifteen offers a year from this type of buyer. It was clear that sale of this site, together with the property to be sold near the Chicago campus, would give us more than enough to complete the lake project. This willingness to sell that land was reinforced when research and development planners from our Technological School decided that the 107 acres were not sufficient for a research park Northwestern University had been planning since 1960; they would need 500–700 acres.

Prior to the first New Trier referendum in May, 1961, we had been contacted regarding the availability of the golf course, but at that time, the land-fill project need was not clear, and the research-park plans were still being contemplated, so that you might say that the land was more definitely "not for sale" then.

In February, 1962, I received a call from Wes Brown, assistant superintendent at New Trier, asking me if the golf course was for sale. New Trier could condemn the land, since it is not being used for academic purposes. We knew that New Trier could condemn 45 acres and leave us with 62 depreciated acres of no value to us. I told Brown that he could inform the Board if they would make an offer for the entire 107 acres I would take it to our board for their consideration. But if they attempted to condemn for part, we would fight it very strenuously. Our lawyers felt that if we could show in court that such condemnation would do serious damage to the value of our remaining acreage that we might win; also I didn't feel that the School Board would condemn land of the university.

About the same time, the Wilmette park district came to see me about the land for recreational purposes; they were seriously interested in the golf course, but didn't need or couldn't afford all 107 acres. I suggested to both the park board and the School Board that they get together and work out a program for buying the property as a whole and dividing it up for their respective needs. This would have made a beautiful high school campus surrounded by a nine-hole golf course on the south and the Forest Preserve on the north. As far as I know, they never met about this.

Hollister papers—"Why We Must Vote 'No' On June 9 If You Want a Second New Trier On a Logical Location, Fairly Priced." According to Sale, the Board attempted to suppress the ad:

> The day we submitted our ad I received a call from Stults, a fellow member of my church, suggesting that we withdraw it. He was not a close friend—he hadn't talked to me before nor since—but that night he was my "best friend." Lloyd Hollister must have told him about the ad, since no one else could have known about it. Stults admitted that the

---

Q. How do you reconcile your statement to Mrs. Hall and Ray Fowler, that the land would be available if an offer was made, with President Miller's two letters to the Board saying, "The land is not now available"?

A. I told Mystic Tape, the Wilmette park district, and the School Board (all were interested in the golf course), that *if they made us an offer* it would be considered; but no one ever made us an offer. We would have even accepted, probably, $23,000 to $24,000 an acre. Instead they all said, "Tell us if it's for sale and then we'll make an offer." We felt that New Trier was not entirely honest about this. If we told them it was for sale, New Trier could condemn the 45 acres they wanted (they could condemn even if we didn't declare the land for sale, but we were confident they wouldn't) and leave us with 62 unusable acres. Therefore we made it an *all or none* offer. We never received an offer from the Board.

In response to the many calls that President Miller and I received about the status of the land, we decided to tell them that the land was not for sale "at this time," implying that tomorrow it may be if the "right" offer is made—a fair price for all 107 acres. This is what President Miller said in his letters to Allen Stults, because we couldn't publicly state that the land was for sale and risk a condemnation procedure for part of the land. However, I personally told Stults (as well as Wesley Brown) that the land was available if they made the right offer. Therefore the Board knew full well that the golf course could be purchased.

We had to have a policy on this; I received about fifty phone calls, as did Dr. Miller—some in the late evening; also the trustees, and Dean Payson Wild. The board of trustees discussed it and decided that if no one made an offer, the land was not "available at this time."

I withdrew my name from the statement Fowler had after conferring with President Miller and decided that such a statement could jeopardize the future of the site regarding condemnation. For the same reason, Trustee McGaw withdrew his statement given to Mrs. Hall.

Board could get the Northwestern University site or Mallenckrodt, but offered weak arguments against using either site. Fowler was also called by a Board member and asked to withdraw the ad. He was elated because they were "worried about us."[45]

But if the Board members were worried, they need not have been. On June 9, 1962, the second referendum to purchase the Northfield site was approved, 12,530 to 6,108, by an electorate which had decided it could not put expansion off any longer.

## A Successful Formula Repeated: The 1963 Building Referendum

Having resolved the controversy over the location of the second high school, the School Board still needed to gain community approval for the sale of bonds to build the school. During the course of the site campaign, the Board had indicated that if the site referendum were approved, a building-bond referendum of $6,000,000 to $8,000,000 would be submitted in the Fall.

But the June site vote was followed by seven months of virtual silence on the issue of the second school. There were spot news items about the progress of the land purchase negotiations (they went smoothly), a report of joint planning sessions between the New Trier and Northfield trustees and staffs, and an article or two concerning the numerous conferences between a New Trier administration-faculty committee and the new school's architects, but there was no information concerning the referendum date or the exact cost of the second New Trier. Residents throughout the District became concerned. Boosters of the School Board were afraid that its failure to communicate its intentions would decrease the public enthusiasm which had been generated during the site campaign and increase voter suspicion of the Board's proce-

[45] Interview with Robert Sale, October 22, 1962.

dures. Residents who were fairly certain of being districted into the new school attendance area began to speculate about the quality of New Trier West, and ponder the possibilities of defeating the referendum if the new plant was not to be equal to the present school. In addition, from November on, there were innumerable rumors spread about the cost of the second school—ranging from $8,000,000 to $11,000,000.

The Board was placed in the precarious position of designing a second school that was equal but not too equal. In order to get the support of those whose children would attend it (or who thought their children would), the school had to appear comparable to New Trier East. But to keep the support of those whose children would continue to attend the old school, it could not be perceived as elaborate. To this task the Board of Education, administration, faculty, and architects applied themselves. The Board had determined that the best chance for a referendum success required that no announcements be made regarding costs until the estimates were complete.

On January 10, 1963, the township voters were informed through the local press that the planned second New Trier would cost $9,430,000, of which $8,750,000 would be requested in a referendum to be held March 9. (Through Board negligence or by design the referendum was delayed until March 16, and then the ten-day advance public notice required by Illinois law was not published.) Anticipating some negative reaction to the estimated cost, Board President Sprowl warned that "plans for the second school can be compared accurately only with the present New Trier, which has a replacement value of about $16,747,210."

Simultaneously, it was announced that the New Trier Information Committee, composed of some of the leading Chicago public relations and advertising executives, was being reactivated for the referendum campaign. An office was opened at the high school, one full-time public relations worker was hired, and it was announced that the committee would accept information requests *twenty-four hours a day*. (Board critic Frances Hall characterized these developments as indicative of "panic behavior" on the part of the School Board.) In addition, the Board, through the Information Committee, arranged with the Hollister papers to run a weekly question-and-answer column confined to second-school issues. Two weeks later, the Committee for Two New Triers, with co-chairmen and block workers in each village, was reactivated to organize support for the referendum.

The Board's referendum announcement, which included detailed facts and figures and artists' sketches of the completed school, converted voter apprehension into general approval. Numerous letters from all District villages appeared in the "Public Forum" praising the Board for designing an "educational twin" for New Trier and urging support for the referendum. The proposal was endorsed by virtually every civic and educational organization in the community (thirty-two in all), including the school boards and parents' organizations of all six elementary school districts, and the influential League of Women Voters. The latter group passed an endorsement resolution after its school cost committee had completed a study of the issue; the committee's report concurred with the School Board's contention that it was impossible to compare the cost of a second New Trier with that of other schools in the area.

Resistance to the proposal was minimal. Those who had been leaders of the "loyal opposition" in 1962 made no overt attempts to block the Board now, since their quarrel with the Board over location had been settled with the June referendum. But, about the time of the building referendum announcement, Roy Pavlik's one-man campaign against School Board "blundering" led him to request Mrs. Hall to bring into the open the unpublished story behind the

Northwestern University site negotiations of the previous May and June. Mrs. Hall conceded that such a disclosure might be used in the public interest, i.e., to make the community aware of "the poor performance of certain Board members" who would be eligible for re-election in April, and to create a more critical concern among district voters for the Board's decisions regarding the cost of the new school. Nevertheless, she decided to remain silent on the matter in order to pursue serious Board consideration of student bus service for both high schools. (She and her husband were co-chairmen of the New Trier Parents' Association Safety Committee.)

The only actual opposition encountered by the Board in 1963 was in the form of seven letters to the "Public Forum," all written by residents who would likely be in the old school attendance area, and who thought the design for the second school was too "plush," or resented what they considered a "snow job" at the taxpayers' expense.[46] The major criticism, however, appeared to be that the cost of the second New Trier would be substantially higher than that of other Chicago-area high schools built recently.

In its several Hollister ads, and one direct mailing, the Board attempted to answer these objections: (a) this is not just a second high school, it is a second New Trier and quality can't be compromised; and (b) quality construction costs more initially but saves money in the long run due to reduced maintenance costs. An independent survey of costs and facilities of new high schools in the area by a Hollister reporter supported the School Board's position. His research indicated that, while other schools had cost less than the proposed New

---

[46] In Illinois, it is legal for school districts to use tax money for "informational" campaigns. Some residents felt, however, that the difference between School Board "propaganda" and educational "information" went unobserved by the Board between 1961 and 1963.

Trier, in every case the announced costs were for a school which was less than complete:

> Several of the schools studied did not include auditoriums or pools. Some of them were built in stages and additional funds will be needed to serve anticipated enrollment. Others included semifinished shells for auditoriums, gymnasiums, and cafeterias, and officials plan to complete these facilities at additional expense.[47]

In addition to justifying the cost of the new school, the Board's ads stressed the high correlation between high educational standards and high property values, as an inducement to those voters whose children would not attend the new school.

The voters of the District were apparently convinced by the Board's design and rationale. The March 16 referendum carried easily, 11,435–3,277, winning approval in each of the eighteen precincts.

## Two New Triers: The School Board Draws a Line

Thus, two and one-half years after determining the need for additional facilities, the New Trier Board of Education had succeeded in gaining voter support for its policy decisions on school location and building cost. In a real sense, the 1963 referendum could be interpreted as the conclusion of a ten-year cycle of disintegration and reintegration within the New Trier community. This notion will be pursued in the following chapter, with the use of referendum voting statistics from 1953, 1957, 1961, 1962, and 1963.

The one decision which the School Board had failed to make palatable to the community, and which was the probable cause of the 1961 site referendum defeat, was its proposal to divide the District into two separate attendance areas. The

[47] *Wilmette Life*, March 7, 1963

Board recognized the necessity of winning the support of those members of the community who feared being segregated in a new school, the quality of which was uncertain. Accordingly, it postponed redistricting until "concerned Township groups [had] a chance to give their opinion" to Board members, who would make a decision "in 1964 or 1965." The Board also adopted and publicized what became known as the "major villages" principle of districting—recognition of the desirability of having students from the major villages (Wilmette, Winnetka, and Glencoe) in both schools. It was hoped that this declaration of intent would satisfy all concerned that no village, section, or group was to be segregated.

But the acceptance of a principle and the drawing of actual lines where no clear geographical boundaries exist are two different matters. By postponing the decision the Board had neglected to resolve a vital issue; this issue, if seriously contested, might precipitate a new round of inter-community conflict and disintegration within the New Trier community. The probability was that the "major villages" principle had been generally well received and could be converted into an acceptable solution without ruffling too many feathers. But having been stunned once by the results of their own presumption, the Board and the superintendent remained apprehensive.

By early November, 1963, Superintendent Cornog and his staff, in consultation with the School Board, had determined that the crisis was imminent: a relatively minor administration procedure, involving student advisor assignments, would necessitate that the District be divided into east and west attendance areas no later than June, 1964. Two days before the announcement of the impending decision appeared in the Hollister papers, a letter was sent to elementary boards of education, superintendents, PTA leaders, village boards, and presidents of the League of Women Voters in the various villages. The letter outlined the reasons for the Board's decision, the timetable to be followed, and the criteria to be employed in drawing the attendance-area boundaries:

> The freshman class that will enter New Trier in September of 1964 will be the only class actually in attendance as a unit in the present school which will be divided between the two schools with the opening of the second high school in the fall of 1965.
>
> Under the New Trier system each entering freshman student is assigned to a faculty advisor group of approximately thirty students, which group remains intact under the aegis of the same faculty advisor throughout the student's four years of high school attendance.
>
> So that the class entering as freshmen next September can be divided between the two high schools by advisor groups when the second school is opened in the fall of 1965, it will be necessary to have the attendance districts for the two schools determined prior to the time the members of this class are initially assigned to their respective advisor groups during the summer of 1964.
>
> For this reason, the Board of Education must formulate the attendance districts for the two schools no later than May or June of 1964. By doing this, each student in next fall's freshman class can be assigned to an advisor group made up entirely of students from his attendance district, thereby making it feasible to divide the class between the two schools at the beginning of its sophomore year without disrupting the make-up or continuity of any advisor group.
>
> However, before arriving at any determination of attendance district lines, the Board of Education is interested in hearing from concerned groups in regard to districting. We shall appreciate receiving a written statement of your views, and if you wish to supplement it with oral comments, a meeting for that purpose has been scheduled for Monday evening, January 27, 1964. . . .[48]

In extending this general invitation to New Trier residents to express their opinions on the question of districting,

---

[48] Letter dated December 10, 1963, signed by New Trier Board President Charles R. Sprowl. Copies of the letter were mailed to members of the defunct New Trier Information Committee and officers of the defunct Citizens for Two New Triers.

the Board stipulated three criteria that would be used in drawing the line. First was a *five-to-seven student ratio* between the two schools; 58 per cent of the District's student body would be assigned to the existing school, and 42 per cent would be assigned to the new school. This ratio was based on the relative capacities of the two physical plants. A second criterion was the Board's intent to honor its previous commitment to the *"major villages" principle*. The third concerned the Board's desire to make *full use of the existing public transportation facilities*.

The response to the Board's invitation came in two forms. The initial reaction was expressed in letters to the New Trier Board of Education from officials of the community's elementary school boards and civic organizations, as well as from a number of interested individuals.[49] Of the fourteen letters received prior to the January 27 redistricting hearing, nine supported the "major villages" principle. These endorsed the idea of using a geographical boundary line rather than dividing students between the two schools on the basis of the existing junior high school attendance areas. Two other respondents emphasized their support of the Board's announced intention of making full use of existing public transportation facilities, but urged that, if necessary for the "safety and well-being of the students," the New Trier District should "go into the transportation business" to provide safe, convenient, and moderate-cost transportation between school and home.[50] Only one letter raised the issue of

[49] This section draws on information contained in Appendix B, "A Summary and Digest of Letters Received on Districting," in *Memo on Districting*, by Robert Harper, administrative assistant to Superintendent William Cornog, New Trier Township High School District, April, 1964.

[50] The New Trier District provided no transportation for its students. Students used a combination of parent- or self-driven automobiles, public buses, and private bus lines provided on a subscription basis. The question of the high school's responsibility for the student transportation, particularly in terms of safety, had been a recurrent one, and was reintroduced by the districting issue.

"sibling-splits," questioning the intention of the Board with regard to "students from the same family [going to] different schools at the same time." Two organizations—the New Trier Parents' Association and the Wilmette League of Women Voters—wrote to express their confidence in the ability of the New Trier Board to solve the districting problem.

The second response took place at the January 27 public hearing. Five of the nine statements received by the Board that night were in the form of proposals and/or criteria for districting. Two of these emphasized the need to be concerned about the integrity of the existing elementary and junior high schools involved in the districting. One suggested a way to minimize the "wrench" which the students of divided junior high graduating classes would experience: these classes should be split as evenly as possible, i.e., by sending 50 per cent to each of the two high schools. In a similar vein, another citizen expressed concern that districting based on geographical lines would "deprive young high school students . . . of the security that results from association with long-time friends and classmates," and suggested utilizing the existing elementary district lines as the basis of the division.

The third proposal came from a Glencoe resident, who expressed an interest in seeing the district divided in such a way that students from "both sides of the [Chicago and Northwestern Railroad] tracks" would have an opportunity "to meet, mingle, and rub elbows" with each other.

> I do hope that when the Board does draw the line, it will take into account this income disparity, and there is an income disparity of some significance between the areas east and west of the tracks. . . .
> I don't want my kids segregated in an extremely wealthy school where all they can talk about at vacation time is how everybody in the class went to Bermuda, the Bahamas, or the Virgin Islands, or Puerto Rico, or Spain or Madagascar. . . .
> I think the more we mix our kids up, the more we expose

them, the more they mingle with different kinds of people, the stronger individuals they are going to be, because the life that they are going to face is not necessarily the sheltered life of the North Shore. . . .

The fourth proposal was one of the two that offered some concrete recommendations for drawing a line between the east and west attendance areas. Using several explicit criteria, including proximity to each high school, "obvious" boundaries (e.g., railroads and major roads), future growth areas, and something referred to as an eastern or western "orientation" of major residential subdivisions, a zigzag north-south boundary line was offered for the Board's consideration.

The fifth proposal was the one which attracted the most attention, for several reasons. For one thing, it was offered by a group of residents who had been active throughout the New Trier controversy, first in contesting the Happ Road (Northfield) site, and later in working on behalf of the adopted referenda as leaders of the Citizens for Two New Triers committee. A second, and perhaps more compelling, explanation of the attention given to this proposal was the considerable amount of research, effort, and thought that had preceded the oral presentation on January 27. The result was a clearly articulated districting proposal, including a boundary line which soon became known as the "Glass line"—for Bradley Glass, who made the presentation. The Glass line was reached on the basis "of statistics of students and where their parents reside at the present time and projecting into 1967, allowing for an 8% factor representing the customary increase in the number of parochial students which will attend the high schools and making adjustments to anticipate the estimated number of new residents in the district, including a consideration for open home sites . . . ."[51]

The Glass proposal was the work of a group consisting of

[51] Quoted from transcript of statement by Bradley Glass at the January 27, 1963, New Trier Board of Education hearing on districting.

a number of citizens from Northfield and one from Glenview. These two sections of the New Trier District were certain to be part of the new school's attendance area. It was felt that if they exercised some responsible leadership in offering a positive proposal based on objective research, they might be able to influence the Board's decision on a districting solution. Two members of the group—Jeremy Beman (Northfield) and J. Stanley Blum (Glenview)—were instrumental in the preparation of the Glass line; but, because of Beman's identification with the earlier conflict over the site selection, and Blum's status as a member of the Wilmette Board of Education, both played *sub rosa* roles. Blum updated the extensive research he had done in 1961 and 1962 in projecting the size and location of the New Trier student body, and made this information available to the Northfield group.

The Glass proposal, the presentation of which benefited from the use of a set of attractive graphic flip charts supplied by Beman, was predicated on the assumption of "substantial representation" from the three major villages. Glass defined this to mean the use of a seven-to-five student ratio for *each* of these villages (i.e., for every seven Wilmette, Winnetka, and Glencoe students who would attend the old school, five would attend the new one). He went on to emphasize, "We feel that it is essential that this vital interest of ours be shared by the people in the major villages, and that the only realistic way to insure their vital interest is through . . . a representative attendance of their children at the new school along [these] lines . . . ."

Other criteria employed in fixing the Glass line included *major* arterial transportation routes and the potential for the development of new transportation to serve both schools, and the expectation that the line drawn in 1964 would be flexible enough to accommodate anticipated population shifts.

At the close of the hearing, Board President Sprowl attempted to lay to rest the numerous rumors that the hearing was perfunctory and that the Board had already determined the boundary to be used in creating attendance areas. "I can assure you the Board has arrived at no conclusion—general or otherwise—as to where the districting line shall be. All we are doing at the present time is assembling factual information and soliciting and receiving . . . recommendations and suggestions."

A reconstruction of the sequence of events between the hearing and the Board's boundary announcement in May tends to confirm Sprowl's statement. Simultaneously with the Board's December announcement regarding its intention to set attendance boundaries by late spring of 1964, Superintendent Cornog's staff began to assemble data of two kinds. One concerned the projection of the size and geographical location of the student population in September, 1967, when the new school would be operating with four grades. This projection was based on a thorough investigation of the number of students in attendance in grades 5, 6, 7, and 8 of the District's *public* schools as of December, 1963, and the area of residence of these students within the District. The staff also assembled data pertaining to the distribution of siblings in New Trier based on the assumption that districting would create "divided families," i.e., families living in the new west attendance area with an older child in old New Trier and a younger sibling attending the new school. Data of both kinds were collected and analyzed by the staff prior to the January 27 Board hearing, but there was no line constructed on the basis of them.

The combination of New Trier staff data, the Glass line and evidence cited to support it, and the expressed concerns of other residents through either written or oral communication with the Board provided the pool of information with which the Board and the New Trier administration worked until the boundary was announced on May 11, 1964. The Glass proposal provided the Board's basic working line, but this underwent some shifts based on the Board's efforts to use existing public transportation insofar as possible (see Figure 4).

To accommodate what were considered legitimate concerns of some segments of the District, the Board announced three school options along with the boundary it established:

> *"Sibling option":* In order to avoid the assignment of children from the same family to two different schools, freshmen from the west area entering New Trier in 1964, 1965, and 1966 who had siblings already enrolled in the east school could opt to attend the east school. Of the approximately 130 students eligible, only 33 per cent had exercised this option as of October, 1964.

> *"Romona Option":* Students who had entered the Romona School (Wilmette) and then the Locust Junior High School (Wilmette) as the oldest student group when those schools were opened would have the option of attending the east school, in order to allow them to mix with older students. Nineteen of the thirty-one children involved so opted as of October, 1964.

> *"Fractional School Option":* Students in each of two junior high school attendance areas divided by the high school boundary were given the option of attending either the high school dictated by their residence or the one attended by the majority of their classmates. This option affected ten students in a west junior high school (Avoca) and fifteen in an east school (Wilmette-Howard). One student (10 per cent) who lived in the east area but attended Avoca opted to go to the new school; 100 per cent of the Howard students living in the west area opted to go to the east school.

The Board felt that the boundary it announced on May 11 met the criteria stipulated the previous December—a 58–

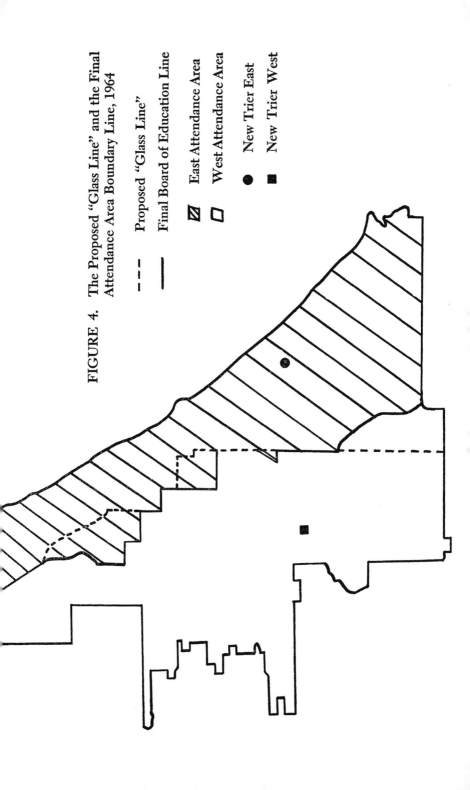

FIGURE 4. The Proposed "Glass Line" and the Final Attendance Area Boundary Line, 1964

- - - Proposed "Glass Line"
——— Final Board of Education Line

▨ East Attendance Area
☐ West Attendance Area

● New Trier East
■ New Trier West

42 per cent east-west student ratio, major-village representation in both schools, and utilization of existing public transportation facilities. Based on a student-population projection
of 4800,[52] the Board's districting line placed 56.5 per cent
(2,711) in the east school and 43.5 per cent (2,089) in the
west.[53] As for major-village representation, Glencoe, Winnetka,
and Wilmette will send 36.5%, 33.8% and 38.3% respectively
to the new school (see Table 4). Utilization of at least one
major existing public transportation route was increased when
the Board shifted the Glass line in west Glencoe and Winnetka to allow more students to make use of the Greenbay
Road bus line, and compensated for this change by moving
the line to the east in Wilmette.

Despite apprehension on the part of the Board and
administration early in the process, the announced district
line was generally well received by the New Trier community.
Not a single letter of dissatisfaction (or satisfaction) appeared
in the "Public Forum" column of the Hollister papers. New
Trier officials reported receipt of numerous compliments on
the "care" and "thoroughness" with which they had
approached districting. One high school administrator
assessed the acceptance of the line in this way:

> The public didn't feel victimized by this line. They knew
> a decision had to be made and they had ample opportunity to
> express their opinions and offer suggestions to those who

[52] The Board of Education's student-population projection was based on
the number of pupils in *public school* grades 5 through 8 as of December,
1963. The Glass-Blum projection for 1967 was 5,647, based on the public
school enrollment "plus an 8% factor to allow for the customary number of
parochial students to attend the high school, [and anticipation of] the
estimated number of new residents in each district, including consideration of
open homesites." The Board recognized these factors, but assumed that their
impact "will be spread over the township rather uniformly and while they may
increase enrollments slightly they will not affect the percentages between the
two schools."

[53] These percentages and numbers do not include switches resulting from
the options outlined above. Seventy-six west-to-east options had been exercised
as of October, 1964; these reduced the percentage of students assigned to the
west school to 41.9, or one-tenth of one per cent below the established goal.

## TABLE 4

### Estimated Allocation of Projected New Trier Student Enrollment, Based on May, 1964, Districting

| | Glencoe | Winnetka | Sunset Ridge | Avoca | ELEMENTARY SCHOOL DISTRICTS Wilmette Locust | Wilmette Howard | Wilmette Total | Kenilworth | Total |
|---|---|---|---|---|---|---|---|---|---|
| Enrollment, grades 5–8 (Dec., 1963) | 914 | 965 | 253 | 521 | (792) | (1,030) | 1,822 | 325 | 4,800 |
| Number assigned to west school | 334 | 326 | 253 | 479 | (654) | (43) | 697 | 0 | 2,089 |
| Number as % of elem. district enrollment | 36.5% | 33.8% | 100% | 91.9% | (82.6%) | (4.2%) | 38.3% | 0% | 43.5% |
| Number as % of west school enrollment | 16.0% | 16.0% | 12.0% | 23.0% | (31.0%) | (2.6%) | 33.0% | 0% | 100.0% |
| Number assigned to east school | 580 | 639 | 0 | 42 | (138) | (987) | 1,125 | 325 | 2,711 |
| Number as % of elem. district enrollment | 63.5% | 66.2% | 0% | 8.1% | (17.4%) | (95.8%) | 61.7% | 100.0% | 56.5% |
| Number as % of east school enrollment | 21.0% | 24.0% | 0% | 2.0% | (5.0%) | (37.0%) | 41.0% | 12.0% | 100.0% |

would make the decision. The public wants to be shown. Its acceptance of this decision indicates what complete preparedness will accomplish.[54]

There was, however, some negative reaction to the boundary, as might be expected whenever a dividing line is drawn. Large sections of the District in both the east and west were well aware before the Board's decision was announced that the "major villages" criterion necessitated a north-south line and that they would fall well inside any such line, and they accepted this probability. The complaints that were voiced came from individual families located on or near the announced line who felt either that the Board's line was arbitrary or that they had sufficient grounds for a waiver. The Board considered each waiver request and granted several, including one to a group of families living on four dead-end streets just west of the line who felt "cut off" from the "east community." This request was first denied, as announced in the Hollister papers on July 16. It was subsequently approved, without explanation. One Board critic observed privately that a member of the Board who had just moved from the District had lived on one of the streets concerned.

Another criticism, also expressed privately, was directed at the Board's "wiggly line" in Glencoe (see Figure 4). The Board's public explanation for the location of this line was put in terms of increasing the use of an existing public bus line. The critic saw it as a reflection of existing ethnic patterns in Glencoe. She felt that the Board had shifted the "Glass line" to the middle of the Skokie Country Club grounds to retain in old New Trier the "old gentile families" residing to the east and north of the golf course. It was noted "parenthetically" that the president of the Board of Education lived on one of the streets retained in the east attendance area by this shift.

Significantly, such criticisms appeared to be few in

[54] Interview with Robert Harper, administrative assistant to Superintendent Cornog, November 5, 1964.

number, and they did not become topics for public discussion. In general, the community reflected satisfaction with the procedure the Board had used in deciding the districting question, and—with the exceptions noted—with the line itself. The Board's previous apprehension over this "issue" proved unwarranted, because in fact districting did not become an issue. Rather, it was an anticlimax to the struggle that had preceded it in the community. The final blueprint for dividing New Trier provided for a majority of the District to remain in the attendance area of the existing school, and left residents therefore relatively unconcerned with districting. And the most vociferous of the earlier critics of the Board's procedures and policies had won victories—the Board had moved in the direction of responsibility and responsiveness, and it had acquiesced to demands that both schools be representative of the District's population.

The problem of drawing the line dividing the District into east and west attendance areas was essentially a mechanical one which most concerned the borderline residents. Through attendance options and a few waivers, all but a few families in either district were accommodated, and the potential of districting as an issue of community conflict was dissipated.

But the potential for conflict in a community is always present. The new school still had to be completed, and to the satisfaction of those in the west attendance area. Perhaps more important for long-term tranquillity in New Trier, a procedure had to be found for electing members of the Board of Education in such a way that the attendance areas created by districting would be fairly represented.

# 3 | Social Disintegration and Integration in a Plural Community: An Analysis of the New Trier Controversy

This chapter attempts to analyze the integration of the New Trier villages in support of a program affecting them all—the proposed expansion policy of the New Trier High School District. The emphasis is on the integrative mechanisms within individual social and political structures, and on the ways in which these operate to make a formally organized plural community viable. Such a community is defined as a group of independent units which have banded together into a larger political system, voluntarily relinquishing a part of their autonomy, in order to increase their collective capability of dealing with an important public problem common to all. Four integrative mechanisms which would increase the probable viability of a plural community are hypothesized—a set of common beliefs concerning the goals of the plural community, the loyalty of the residents to both the primary and plural units, an effective two-way communications network, and cosmopolitan leadership.

In this study the New Trier High School District has been described as a formally organized, uni-functional plural community comprising five suburban villages. The empirical evidence of New Trier's ten-year (1953–63) effort to expand its high school facilities to meet the community's increased needs will be used, along with an analytic framework consisting of the four hypothesized variables, to examine the process of suburban socio-political integration.

## Integration, Disintegration, and Reintegration

It has been submitted above (Chapter Two) that the postwar events in the New Trier community reveal a theme of social integration, disintegration, and reintegration. A close examination of the five expansion referenda since 1953 confirms this impression.

From the organization of the New Trier District in 1899 until the end of World War II, the people and villages composing it formed a homogeneous community. Socio-economic status was relatively high throughout the community, the desirability of a quality educational system was uniformly accepted, and support for District policies designed to achieve educational excellence was strong. Every tax-rate increase that was proposed and every bond referendum that was held in the District during that period was overwhelmingly approved, and not one School Board election was contested. Socially and politically, as well as constitutionally, the New Trier community was integrated through its first half-century of being.

But postwar social and demographic changes in the structure of the Chicago metropolitan area created disintegrative forces and a potential for social conflict within the New Trier community. The township population, which had grown only 3 per cent between 1940 and 1950, increased 42.3 per cent in the following decade. Population growth brought concomitant changes in the social structure, resulting in a less homogeneous community. Thus, at the same time that population growth made necessary new or expanded school facilities, growing socio-economic differentiation within the electorate made it increasingly difficult to gain public support for the Board of Education's expansion policies.

Compounding the difficulty of achieving consensus was the failure of the District's governing body to recognize the social changes that were taking place, and to alter its strategy accordingly. In the past, the New Trier community had always accepted school policy unquestioningly. Postwar School Boards operated on the premise that such was still the case (until after the 1961 referendum defeat), even when the Board's 1957 expansion proposition was soundly rejected. In short, there was little overt effort on the part of the Board to create a consensus for its policies within a changing community.

Furthermore, the transition from Superintendent Matthew Gaffney's twenty-three-year administration (1931–54) to the new administration under William Cornog presented the Board with a problem of role uncertainty which was not easily resolved. Gaffney had been a good politician as well as a good administrator and educator. He had won the confidence of the people and the Board during his tenure, and virtually was able to dictate policy and have it accepted without question. When Gaffney retired in 1954, the leadership gap thus created was filled by neither his successor nor the Board of Education. One New Trier resident put it this way:

> Matt Gaffney made New Trier. He was everything to everybody. He made all the decisions—most were good ones—and the public depended on him. The Board's role was vestigial; they were nice people but they didn't do anything. When Cornog took over, the Board didn't know what it was supposed to do. Cornog was very capable, but he looked to the Board to do their job. He looked for leadership but never got it. For the first time, New Trier was faced by a major issue, and the Board should have faced up to it when Cornog arrived, but it was swept under the rug. They felt they could always expand the school. The Board felt that the old school would never get too crowded, and besides, the public wanted to stay in the old school; there was social stigma attached to leaving it.[1]

[1] Interview with J. Stanley Blum, November 28, 1962.

The 1953 decision to spend $5,000,000 to expand old New Trier was Gaffney's last major decision, and in retrospect, according to most long-time residents, his only bad one. Although there was some agitation for a second high school at that time, Gaffney did not foresee, or did not want to foresee, the population problem that was developing. He had established a national reputation for *the* New Trier High School, and he did not want to see that institution divided between two campuses. In 1953 the population growth was just beginning, and the social distance between residents was still small. Gaffney's expansion decision was validated by the voters without serious opposition.

The overwhelming support given the 1953 referendum (it carried easily in each precinct throughout the District) suggests that the New Trier community was still well integrated at that time. Such a degree of community integration was not again achieved in the District until 1963, when the $8,750,000 school bond proposal carried in all eighteen precincts. Between 1953 and 1963, the New Trier District experienced social and political disintegration and a gradual process of community reintegration. This ten-year cycle can be clearly observed in Table 5.

The unexpected rejection of the Board of Education's 1961 proposal to buy the Northfield property as a site for a second high school has been presented above in some detail. This rejection resulted from the introduction of two new variables into the New Trier political system—loss of confidence in the system's decision makers, and social change within the community—and from reinforcement of a third—strong village allegiance.

(a) *Loss of confidence in the decision makers:* Although the School Board's costly 1953 expansion referendum was endorsed overwhelmingly by the community, seeds of doubt concerning the wisdom of this decision were planted by the small but vocal minority which preferred a second high school. The majority, however, satisfied that New Trier had

## TABLE 5

Community Support for Postwar New Trier Referenda,
by Per Cent of Total Vote, and Per Cent of Precincts

|  | 1953 | 1957 | 1961 | 1962 | 1963 |
|---|---|---|---|---|---|
| % total vote supporting referendum | 71.8 | 18.9 | 44.0 | 67.2 | 81.7 |
| % precincts supporting referendum | 100.0 (7)[a] | 0.0 (8)[a] | 35.7 (14)[a] | 83.3 (18)[a] | 100.0 (18)[a] |

[a] The number of precincts varied in all but the 1962 and 1963 referenda; the figures in parentheses indicate the number of precincts at the time of each referendum.

won national recognition through the leadership and policy decisions of the superintendent and school trustees, accepted their solution to what was expected to be a short-term population problem. But when high school enrollment exceeded the expanded capacity of the enlarged facilities by the time the new buildings were dedicated in 1957,[2] discontent with the 1953 decision and the officials responsible for it became more widespread.

The Board of Education did nothing to improve its relationship with the community when, in 1957, it literally threatened to condemn the homes of thirty families adjacent to the high school in order to convert into playground space the seven acres occupied by the homes. Although there were a few public expressions of confidence in the judgment of the decision makers at that time, statements of dissatisfaction and resentment were common throughout the District. In addition to those who opposed the Board's plan on moral or procedural grounds, or both, there was a larger group who felt that the Board's proposal would compound the mistake made in 1953 by attempting to expand by means of additional

[2] Enrollment in 1953 was 2,500; the enlarged facilities were designed to house 3,000 students with space to expand to 3,500. Enrollment in 1957 was 3,400, and the following year, 3,650.

construction on an already-crowded site. The solution advocated by these residents was a second high school. Thus a community which hitherto had accepted school policy decisions readily now seriously questioned the judgment and foresight of its governing body. The result was a humiliating defeat for the Board of Education, in which only 19 per cent of the community supported its plan. The 1957 defeat was the more bitter for the Board because it was the first in fifty-eight years, and because it forced the Board to retreat from its audacious strategy of proceeding with the plan regardless of the referendum outcome.

But it took the New Trier Board a second referendum defeat in 1961 to learn that the community had become disenchanted with the oligarchic process of making major policy decisions. In the first place, the Board's failure to act on the enrollment crisis until it was an actuality had antagonized the public. The saturation point (3,500 students) for the high school facilities was surpassed in the fall of 1958, but the decision to build a second school was not reached until February, 1961. By then the enrollment had reached 4,250, with a projection of 5,000 before the school could be completed.

Secondly, the manner in which the second-school decision was reached caused considerable resentment in the District. Both the decision to build a second four-year high school and the selection of the site in Northfield were made by the Board (in consultation with the administration) *without* reference to community opinion. Only after the decisions were made and publicized was there an attempt by the Board to solicit support. This attempt failed largely because there was little basis for consensus under the circumstances: social disparity within the population was being compounded by the very nature of the Board's proposal, i.e., by the suggested geographical separation of the functional community into two distinct parts. The Board, in essence, was proposing the fragmentation of the one integrative element in the community—*the* New Trier High School, complete with its tradition, prestige, and reputation—without seriously considering the divisive consequences of its decision. One School Board trustee, when questioned about the decision, replied proudly, "The Board decided on the basis of educational value only, not on what the community would accept; the latter had no part in the Board's thinking."

But the outcome of the 1961 referendum suggests that the Board's evaluation of community willingness to accept its solution to the problem of school overcrowding was much too optimistic. First, the community was hesitant about accepting the Board's solution because it was dissatisfied with the previous "solutions" to the same problem in 1953 and 1957. One Winnetka resident expressed this attitude succinctly: "We believed the Board in 1953 and enlarged the High School at a cost of $6,000,000 and seven years later we learned how incompetent they were. Are we to believe the present Board is any more competent?"[3]

Second, the issue of one large versus two smaller schools, or indeed, of whether a possible second high school should contain one, two, or four grades, had not been adequately deliberated to convince the community that the Board's proposal was the best possible solution. After all, argued a number of citizens, the Cornog-Brown Report[4] gave convincing arguments for and against *all* the alternatives, including the one finally decided on by the Board of Education.

Third, it was felt that the Board had made and announced its choice of a site for the second school without attempting to weigh the consequences of the decision. In addition to being incensed over their exclusion from the deliberations on site, the vocal public resented the Board's failure to communicate its criteria for selection of the Northfield site,

---

[3] *Wilmette Life*, May 18, 1961.
[4] William Cornog and Wesley Brown, "A Cursory Examination of the Several Proposals for Additional New Trier Township High School Building" (5 pp., mimeo.; New Trier Township High School, Dec. 15, 1960).

cost data, and other information which would have made it possible to cast an intelligent vote. Further, and perhaps more significant, was the Board's failure to appreciate the effect that choosing a site in the western part of the District would have on intercommunity relations. One Board member, attempting to stress the objectivity with which the Board acted, declared somewhat boastfully that "the village in which the school would be located was not a consideration in the selection of the site; any suitable site was acceptable [to the Board]." But the choice of a location in the westernmost village would require an east-west split of the District; and when the proposed attendance-area line was announced, it was interpreted by the western "newcomers" as an attempt by the eastern residents to segregate them from the rest of the District. The fact that only one of the seven Board trustees was from the western section of the District did nothing to increase confidence in the decision that had been made.[5] The residents of Northfield further opposed the decision on grounds that it would remove property from the tax rolls and would also be costly in terms of services to be provided. They felt Northfield had been selected as the location of the new school because it was too small to fight back. Nor did Northfielders welcome the "opportunity" to be housed in the same high school as the residents of west Wilmette; the "cultural and social aspirations" incident created strong antagonism between west Wilmette and Northfield and exacerbated the east-west division of opinion.[6]

---

[5] The trustee from Northfield was the only member who opposed the 1961 decision, and at that, not publicly. There was strong pressure to have the Board appear unanimous.

[6] The Northfield Board representative interpreted the Northfield–west Wilmette conflict in this way: "The 'anti-Semitic thing' was not the real concern in the controversy. Northfield used the Jewish argument to cover up the concern they felt at being cut off from Winnetka, to which they feel extremely strong ties. . . . The first referendum districting absolutely cut off Northfield from Winnetka with regard to New Trier where all these other ties existed. This hurt." (Interview, November 30, 1961.)

(b) *Social change within the New Trier community*: Both the Northfield–west Wilmette incident and the more general east-west conflict of 1961 resulted from a second major cause of community disintegration between 1953 and 1961— social change. It was noted above that the New Trier District experienced a sharp rise in population during the 1950–60 decade which increased the number of residents by approximately one-half (42,636 to 64,020). The prior saturation of the District's eastern area—Winnetka, Kenilworth, east Wilmette, and east Glencoe—forced a concentration of the newcomers into the less developed western part of the township. Table 6 indicates the growth areas.

Not only was there a significant increase in the size of the New Trier community by 1960; there was also a perceptible change in its social structure. The people moving into the western section of the District tended to be somewhat different from the eastern residents. Table 7 indicates that, while the educational level is uniformly high throughout the community, eastern residents are, in general, wealthier and are employed in occupations conferring more prestige than those residing in the western area.

One difference between east and west New Trier which came into sharp focus during the 1961 referendum, and which apparently was a strong disintegrative force, was one for which there are no census data, viz., religious affiliation. In addition to being newcomers to the District, large numbers of the west Wilmette residents were eastern European Jews; they were thus differentiated not only from the District's predominantly Protestant population, but also from the wealthier and more socially acceptable (in New Trier) German Jews in Glencoe. Many of the Catholic residents, who generally opposed increased tax rates for public schools, were also concentrated in west Wilmette.

Social change—population growth and differentiation—had important consequences for School Board expan-

# TABLE 6

Population Increases in New Trier Township
High School District, 1950–60,
by Attendance Area and Census Tract[a]

| East New Trier | | | |
|---|---|---|---|
| **Census Tract** | | **Population** | **% Inc.** |
| Number | Village | 1950 | 1960 | 1950–60 |
| NTT-1 | E. Glencoe | 2,369 | 2,955 | 24.7 |
| NTT-2 | W. Glencoe | 4,611 | 7,517 | 63.0 |
| NTT-3 | E. Winnetka | 4,061 | 4,318 | 6.3 |
| NTT-4 | N. W. Winnetka | 3,194 | 3,751 | 17.4 |
| NTT-5 | S. W. Winnetka | 4,850 | 5,299 | 9.2 |
| NTT-6 | Kenilworth | 2,789 | 2,959 | 6.0 |
| NTT-7 | E. Wilmette | 3,207 | 3,572 | 11.3 |
| NTT-8 | E. Wilmette | 4,359 | 4,739 | 8.7 |
| Total | | 29,440 | 35,110 | 19.2 |
| West New Trier | | | |
| NTT-9 | C. Wilmette | 5,414 | 5,493 | 1.4 |
| NTT-10 | S. W. Wilmette | 2,072 | 8,953 | 332.0 |
| NTT-11 | N. W. Wilmette | 3,110 | 5,263 | 69.2 |
| | Northfield[b] | 1,426 | 4,005 | 180.9 |
| NTT-13 | Glenview | 584 | 2,651 | 357.4 |
| Total | | 12,606 | 26,365 | 109.1 |

[a] Source: *United States Census of Population and Housing: 1960 Census Tracts* (Final Reports, PHC[1]–26; Washington, D.C.: United States Government Printing Office, 1962).
[b] Northfield was not tracted by the Bureau of the Census in 1950: The figures used here are for the municipality of Northfield, which includes most of tracts NTT-0012 and NFT-0046.

sion proposals because it divided the community into east and west factions. The east-west dichotomy was manifested along four lines—native-newcomer, rich–less rich, Jew-Protestant, and Eastern European Jew–German Jew. Until the Board of Education proposed a second four-year high school for the District and drew boundaries accentuating these differences, the division remained latent. Thereafter it became real for both factions. The "natives" saw the Board's proposal as an opportunity to give the newer arrivals, whose migration to the community, they felt, had caused school overcrowding, "a

## TABLE 7

### Socio-economic Differences within New Trier Township High School District, by Attendance Area and Census Tract, 1960[a]

| | | East New Trier | | |
| --- | --- | --- | --- | --- |
| Census Tract[b] | Village | % Pop. 25 yrs + w/ HS+ Educ. | % Families w/ Income $25,000+ | % Occupations Prof'l/Mgr'l |
| NTT-1 | E. Glencoe | 82.7 | 47.7 | 51.1 |
| NTT-2 | W. Glencoe | 58.7 | 33.6 | 50.6 |
| NTT-3 | E. Winnetka | 68.3 | 40.6 | 52.5 |
| NTT-4 | N. W. Winnetka | 70.4 | 39.5 | 57.4 |
| NTT-5 | S. W. Winnetka | 62.0 | 37.5 | 50.3 |
| NTT-6 | Kenilworth | 68.8 | 45.0 | 65.5 |
| NTT-7 | E. Wilmette | 64.7 | 42.5 | 57.4 |
| NTT-8 | E. Wilmette | 79.4 | 15.6 | 50.9 |
| Mean | | 68.6 | 40.1 | 51.8 |
| | | West New Trier | | |
| NTT-9 | C. Wilmette | 66.2 | 6.5 | 37.5 |
| NTT-10 | S. W. Wilmette | 74.8 | 8.9 | 45.9 |
| NTT-11 | N. W. Wilmette | 82.9 | 30.4 | 58.2 |
| NTT-12 | Northfield | 67.2 | 27.2 | 41.8 |
| NFT-46 | Northfield | 63.0 | 18.0 | 55.5 |
| NTT-13 | Glenview | 58.6 | 13.3 | 49.0 |
| Mean | | 66.7 | 15.7 | 47.5 |

[a] Data adapted from *United States Census of Population and Housing: 1960 Census Tracts* (Final Report, PHC[1]–26; Washington, D.C.: U.S. Government Printing Office, 1962).
[b] See Figure 5 for the area included in each census tract.

school of their own," and at the same time relieve the pressure on old New Trier. The newcomers, on the other hand, saw it as an attempt by the Board of Education, biased in favor of the older residents, to provide "separate but equal" facilities and thereby segregate them from the community they had worked so hard to join. They seemed less concerned about the educational value of the Board's proposal than about the social wall that it would have erected between them and the

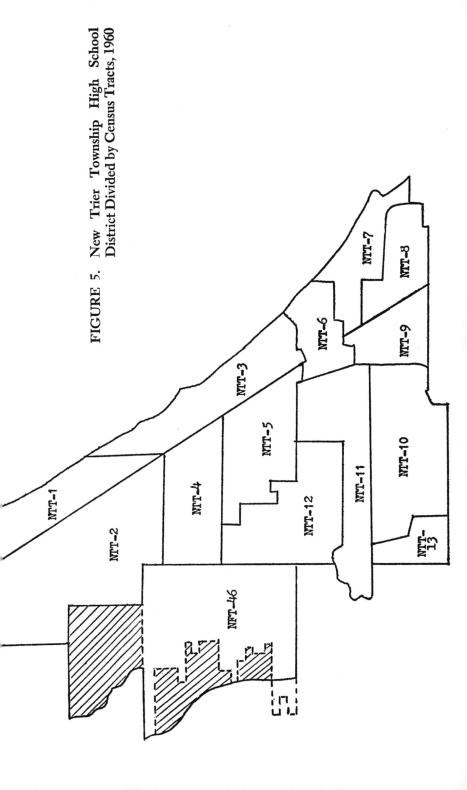

FIGURE 5. New Trier Township High School
District Divided by Census Tracts, 1960

status and prestige of the eastern villages. In general, the 1961 referendum proposal was evaluated less in terms of educational costs and benefits than in terms of social costs and benefits.

Comments by key community actors in an *ex post facto* analysis of the controversy make clear the existence of a perceived difference between east and west New Trier. Said one Board trustee:

> The "no" vote was based not on educational reasons but on a "look what you're doing to me" reaction. It was a religious question; the west Wilmette Jews wanted to go to school with the higher-status Glencoe Jews. They didn't care about the gentiles. There are two kinds of Jews involved and those in west Wilmette felt they were being separated from the others.

And another member of the Board:

> Glencoe is an old established community with an established Jewish population. They're different from the west Wilmette Jews—they have higher incomes and consider themselves "natives." It was more a question of native versus new and rich versus poor Jews than it was Jew versus gentile.

An officer of the joint New Trier League of Women Voters committee which intensively studied the expansion proposals asserted:

> [The east-west division] wasn't and isn't a case of race; the people in west Wilmette are just a different kind of people. West Wilmette has the only tract houses in the District and they are less expensive than most. We have relatively inexpensive houses in the older sections of Wilmette and Winnetka, but these are owned by people who will take care of them and fix them up.

An active opponent of the Board also evaluated the defeat in terms of the east-west split:

> This is hearsay, but there are social-economic-ethnic differences in New Trier Township. The Board set out to get

a certain group—the Jews from west Wilmette—into the new school. The districting plan made this clear; it was ridiculous. It antagonized many residents and the referendum failed.

And the man who had been chairman of the Citizens' Advisory Committee stated:

> The Jewish influx was under the whole problem. How do you deal rationally with people over schools when they get overemotional regarding *who* is in which school? Although the Jewish "problem" never came out into the open, you could feel it all the time; it underlay the whole thing.

The east-west division was further complicated by a conflict within the western area between Northfield and west Wilmette, precipitated by the "social and cultural aspirations" comment. Both groups resented being segregated from the eastern villages and both voted against the Board's proposal, but for different reasons. Northfielders objected to having their ties with Winnetka severed and to being placed in a school which, it was estimated, would be 60 per cent Jewish;[7] west Wilmette residents, on the other hand, were opposed to sending their children to a high school which would be permeated by "subterfuge, prejudice, and social tension."

The precinct map (Figure 6) and voting statistics for the 1961 referendum (Table 8) clearly show the east-west schism created in the community by the School Board's proposed solution to the problem of overcrowded facilities. In only one precinct scheduled to remain in the old school's attendance area was the referendum defeated.

(c) *Strong village allegiance:* A third force operating to divide the New Trier political community over school expansion was the existence of a stronger resident identification

[7] A Northfield opposition leader felt that this position was not anti-Semitic: "My concern was not with the Jewish element; it was based on the inequality of the two school populations that will result." Assured by the Board's "major villages" policy in 1962, he became a staunch supporter of the second site referendum.

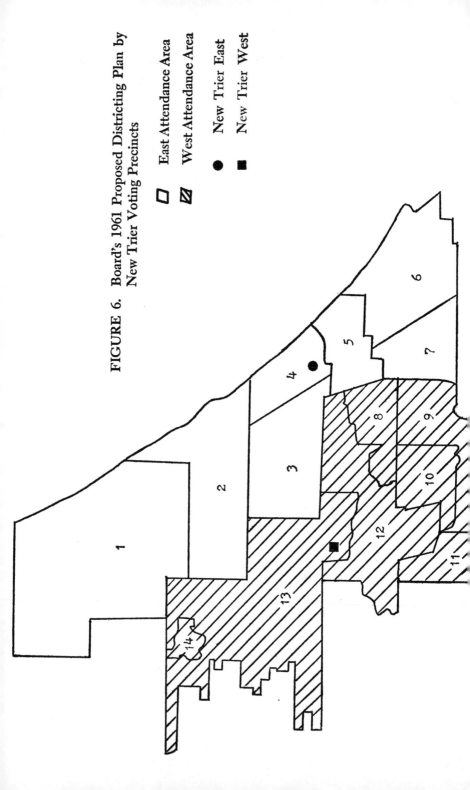

FIGURE 6. Board's 1961 Proposed Districting Plan by New Trier Voting Precincts

☐ East Attendance Area

▨ West Attendance Area

● New Trier East

■ New Trier West

with the primary community—the village—than with the plural community. The one possible exception was Wilmette, where the rapid influx of relatively low-income residents into the western half of the long, narrow village had caused an east-west split *within* the municipality. An east Wilmette resident put it this way:

> A definite east-west split has developed. They [east and west Wilmette] are too far apart. We have little interaction with them; they drive to Chicago via the Edens Expressway and we commute on the [Chicago &] Northwestern Railroad. And there are religious differences, which eliminates the church as a focus of interaction.

The relative strength of village loyalties within the New Trier community manifested itself in a number of ways during the expansion controversy. One indicator of this strength was the vigorous opposition of some residents to location of the new facility in *their* village. Many non-Northfielders were disappointed when Northfield vehemently opposed the 1961 site referendum. They thought that any village should be proud to host a high school bearing the "New Trier" label, and particularly a village that had successfully petitioned for

## TABLE 8

### Community Support of 1961 Site Referendum by Precinct and Proposed Attendance Areas

| East New Trier Attendance Area | | | West New Trier Attendance Area | | |
|---|---|---|---|---|---|
| Precinct Number | Village | Percentage "yes" votes | Precinct Number | Village | Percentage "yes" votes |
| 1 | Glencoe | 60.1 | 8 | Wilmette | 29.2 |
| 2 | Winnetka | 60.2 | 9 | Wilmette | 25.4 |
| 3 | Winnetka | 55.8 | 10 | Wilmette | 33.9 |
| 4 | Winnetka | 64.6 | 11 | Glenview | 35.1 |
| 5 | Kenilworth | 58.0 | 12 | Wilmette | 36.0 |
| 6 | Wilmette | 50.4 | 13 | Northfield | 17.0 |
| 7 | Wilmette | 43.3 | 14 | Northbrook | 30.2 |

inclusion in the New Trier District. But Northfielders argued that the integrative costs which would be levied upon the village were too high, especially in terms of tax losses.

The abortive 1962 attempt to locate the second facility in Winnetka also tends to confirm the village-loyalty thesis. The Citizens' Study Committee's recommendation of the "ideal" village-owned Willow-Hibbard site in Winnetka, following the 1961 referendum defeat, elicited immediate statements of disapproval; after an acrimonious town meeting, the village board of trustees refused to sell the land to the high school. Winnetka's opposition was stated in terms of future village needs and the increased burden which a second high school would place on the village. Winnetkans readily suggested that the second school should be put "where it belongs"—in Wilmette, which supplied over 40 per cent of the New Trier student body. The Winnetka attitude toward the proposal was summed up by the resident who declared that it was "good for the township but bad for Winnetka and we should oppose it." Here, too, the integrative cost of the proposal was deemed too high.

But village allegiance works both ways, as the unsuccessful efforts of some Wilmette residents to get the new school located in Wilmette illustrates. A number of Wilmettans agreed with the Winnetkans who argued for a Wilmette location of the second school, on the grounds that a village of Wilmette's size (28,000 in 1960) should have its own facility and determine its own educational policy. The Board of Education, however, did not feel there was a suitable location in Wilmette. There was some talk in Wilmette that the village should withdraw from the New Trier District and form its own high school district, but it was quickly pointed out that to build an adequate facility for Wilmette's students would cost considerably more than the municipality's bonded indebtedness ceiling would provide. Thus further consideration of this alternative was pointless.

Members of the New Trier Board of Education, commenting on the nature of the "New Trier community," summed up the relationship of the villages to the District in this way:

> The referenda have shown the "separateness" of the villages; the resident's loyalty is to his village and not to New Trier. New Trier High School is the *only* unifying factor in the township because no one pays any attention to township government.

> The New Trier District is not a homogeneous community; the high school is the *only* thing that holds it together.

> It has never been a coherent community; the villages simply co-operated in providing a high school. They are very vocal about their autonomy.

## The Integration of a Plural Community

The remainder of this chapter will be concerned with the process of integration—or more accurately, reintegration—within the New Trier community after the east-west division over the 1961 site referendum. The operational definition of community integration is the percentage change in proportion of affirmative votes between 1961 and 1962. Fortunately for purposes of the analysis to be made here, the site propositions voted on in 1961 and 1962 were identical, except for the amount of the estimated bond issue, which had *doubled* in 1962 (to $1,825,000) due to rezoning of the site property. A significant increase in the proportion of voters supporting the proposition in 1962 would support the hypothesis that integration had taken place among the New Trier communities.

A comparison of the 1962 referendum vote with that of the previous year reveals that the expansion had become a cogent issue for a larger proportion of the New Trier electorate. The number voting in 1962 (18,638) was 56.5 per cent higher than the 1961 figure (11,907), increasing the proportion of estimated eligible voters (36,000) who participated from one-third to one-half. This participation increase produced a 139.4 per cent increase in the number of affirmative votes in 1962, and an 8.4 per cent decrease in negative votes. Or, to put it another way, the *number* of those opposed to the expansion proposition remained relatively constant (6,675 in 1961; 6,108 in 1962), while the number in favor of it more than doubled. In the absence of panel interviews with voters, it is impossible to ascertain individual vote changes, but it can be inferred from precinct results in the two referenda that the School Board's 1962 "hard sell" campaign had little effect on those who had voted negatively in 1961, but was highly successful in reinforcing the supportive voters and converting 1961 non-voters into "yes" voters.

Table 9 shows that the number of "no" votes remained

## TABLE 9

### Change in Frequency of "No" Votes, 1961–62, by Precinct

| Precinct | "No" Votes | | Difference | Percentage Change |
| | 1961 | 1962 | | |
|---|---|---|---|---|
| 1 | 550 | 636 | +86 | +15.6 |
| 2 | 403 | 302 | −101 | −25.0 |
| 3 | 445 | 608 | +163 | +36.6 |
| 4 | 248 | 211 | −37 | −14.9 |
| 5 | 271 | 215 | −56 | −20.6 |
| 6 | 682 | 609 | −73 | −10.7 |
| 7 | 470 | 471 | +1 | +0.2 |
| 8 | 550 | 378 | −172 | −31.2 |
| 9 | 523 | 514 | −9 | −1.7 |
| 10 | 442 | 273 | −169 | −38.2 |
| 11 | 328 | 311 | −17 | −5.1 |
| 12 | 475 | 406 | −69 | −14.5 |
| 13 | 1,244 | 1,135 | −109 | −8.7 |
| 14 | 44 | 39 | −5 | −11.3 |
| Total | 6,675 | 6,108 | −567 | −8.4 |

about the same or *decreased* in twelve of the fourteen precincts, including the seven western precincts in which the 1961 proposal had been rejected. The two precincts (in Glencoe and Winnetka) in which the frequency of "no" votes increased significantly were ones which anticipated being included in the new school's attendance area under the "major villages" policy of redistricting.

Table 10 represents the most impressive evidence available to support the hypothesis that community integration occurred between 1961 and 1962. With the two referendum proposals controlled (except for the site-cost increase in 1962, which would have tended to *increase* opposition), the pro-

## TABLE 10

### Change in Proportion "Yes" Vote, 1961–62, by Precinct, by Attendance Area, and for Total District

| Precinct Number | | % Yes 1961 | % Yes 1962 | % Difference 1961–62 |
|---|---|---|---|---|
| 1 | (Glencoe) | 60.1 | 79.2 | +19.1 |
| 2 | (Winnetka) | 60.2 | 81.6 | +21.4 |
| 3 | (Winnetka) | 55.8 | 66.0 | +10.2 |
| 4 | (Winnetka) | 64.6 | 80.5 | +15.9 |
| 5 | (Kenilworth) | 58.0 | 78.3 | +20.3 |
| 6 | (Wilmette) | 50.4 | 69.6 | +19.2 |
| 7 | (Wilmette) | 43.3 | 66.0 | +22.7 |
| 1–7 Subtotal | | 55.8 | 74.5 | +18.7 |
| *West New Trier Attendance Area* | | | | |
| 8 | (Wilmette) | 29.2 | 64.4 | +35.2 |
| 9 | (Wilmette) | 25.4 | 49.5 | +24.1 |
| 10 | (Wilmette) | 33.9 | 70.7 | +36.8 |
| 11 | (Wilmette and uninc.) | 35.1 | 63.1 | +28.0 |
| 12 | (Glenview) | 36.0 | 60.2 | +24.2 |
| 13 | (Northfield) | 17.0 | 32.1 | +15.1 |
| 14 | (Northbrook) | 30.2 | 58.9 | +28.7 |
| 8–14 Subtotal | | 27.1 | 54.1 | +27.0 |
| District Total | | 44.0 | 67.2 | +23.2 |

portion of voters supporting the expansion proposition in 1962 increased from 44.0 to 67.2 per cent, an increase of 23.2 per cent. Increased support was evidenced in *each* of the fourteen precincts, with an increase range of 15.1 to 36.8 per cent.[8] Despite increases in the proportion of "yes" votes of 15.1 and 24.1 in Northfield and West Wilmette respectively, the 1962 referendum was defeated in those two precincts, although by only 11 votes of the 1,017 cast in the latter. An analysis of the 1962 vote in terms of the 1961 east-west schism reveals the integrative process that took place (see Table 10). The seven eastern precincts, which, with the exception of one in Wilmette, had provided most of what support there was in 1961, increased their proportion of the "yes" vote from 55.8 to 74.5 per cent. The western precincts, whose 1961 vote was only 27.1 per cent supportive, doubled that figure, to 54.1 per cent, in 1962. The Tenth Precinct (in Wilmette), which is largely Jewish, made the biggest comeback, increasing its percentage of support from 33.9 to 70.7.

In sum, if it is granted that the New Trier plural community was in a state of disintegration following the 1961 referendum defeat, and if measures of integration presented above are accepted, it follows that integrative mechanisms were operating in the community between May, 1961, and June, 1962. In the following section, these mechanisms will be analyzed.

## Integrative Mechanisms in a Plural Community

To understand the significant difference in outcomes of essentially similar referendum proposals in 1961 and 1962, one must examine closely the impact of the 1961 defeat on the New Trier community. North, Koch, and Zinnes have

[8] Between 1961 and 1962, the number of voting precincts was increased from fourteen to eighteen by dividing Glencoe into four precincts and Northfield into two. For purposes of comparative analysis here, however, the 1961 precincts are used.

suggested that social conflict often performs integrative as well as disintegrative functions.[9] The present case affords an opportunity to examine this proposition, in the process of analyzing the operation of the four community integrative mechanisms hypothesized in this study—common values concerning the goals of the plural community, multiple loyalties, an effective communications network, and cosmopolitan leadership.

(a) *Common values concerning community goals:* Despite the defeat of the 1961 expansion proposal, both opponents and proponents of the *specific* plan submitted by the Board of Education—a four-year high school located in Northfield—were in accord on the *general* goal of the plan—the maintenance of a high quality educational system in New Trier. The long-time residents were proud of New Trier's national reputation and did not wish to see it dissipated. Others feared the effect which a decline in educational quality might have on property values in the community. Many of the newer residents had moved to the New Trier area largely so that their children might attend an especially good school. In fact, many who voted against the 1961 referendum did so because they were unconvinced that the Board's proposed departure from the traditional organization of the New Trier District would preserve the quality of the system. The Board had asked the voters to approve a package referendum, which included the three distinct items of a second four-year school, a new location, and high cost, without prior public discussion of its relative merits. Any voter who appreciated the need for expanded facilities but objected to any or all of the three items in the package had no choice but to vote against the proposal.

One integrative function performed by the 1961 referendum defeat was to make it quite clear to the Board of Educa-

[9] Robert C. North, Howard E. Koch, Jr., and Dina A. Zinnes, "The Integrative Functions of Conflict," *The Journal of Conflict Resolution,* IV (Sept., 1960), 355–74.

tion that the social composition of the District had changed, and that approval of major school policy would require the Board, for the first time, to make a concerted effort to create consensus on means despite the existence of community agreement on general goals.

By capitalizing on another common community value—respect for technical expertise—the Board was able to reduce the intensity of the conflict over certain issues before the second referendum. The Real Estate Research Corporation's population-projection study made the one-versus-two school question moot in 1962. The superintendent's declaration, abetted by evidence compiled by the Citizens' Study Committee, that a four-year second school was more sound educationally than a freshman or freshman-sophomore school vitiated this problem as a basis for conflict. Furthermore, once the need for expanded facilities was accepted, the cost issue lost much of its potential divisive power for all the alternatives were expensive. (Many residents, nevertheless, retained a keen sense of dissatisfaction with the District's policy makers, who had shown a lack of foresight concerning expansion needs when land was less expensive.) Finally, the location of the 1962 site, although the same as in 1961, was based on a thorough review of possible alternatives by the Citizens' Study Committee, and was ultimately selected on the basis of availability.

The effectiveness of this strategy of technical consultation is shown by the results of a sample survey made two months before the 1962 referendum. In this survey, 70 per cent of the respondents agreed that a second four-year high school was needed.

The reduction in the intensity and number of issues in conflict, when combined with the basic community regard for high educational standards, enhanced the probability of voter approval in 1962. This probability was further increased by the forced-option nature of the decision to be made by the

## TABLE 11

### Response by Village Concerning Need for Second Four-Year High School, April, 1962[a]

|  | % Yes | % No | % Not Sure | % No Answer | N |
|---|---|---|---|---|---|
| Glencoe | 79 | 6 | 13 | 2 | 128 |
| Winnetka | 79 | 4 | 14 | 3 | 185 |
| Kenilworth | 83 | — | 17 | — | 24 |
| Wilmette | 63 | 12 | 22 | 3 | 385 |
| Northfield | 67 | 11 | 20 | 2 | 56 |
| Glenview | 60 | 11 | 21 | 8 | 38 |
| District | 70 | 9 | 18 | 3 | 827[b] |

[a] Source: New Trier Information Committee. Questionnaire designed by A. C. Nielsen Company and conducted by volunteer residents from New Trier in co-operation with the chief statistician's office and the public relations department of Illinois Bell Telephone Company.
[b] Includes eleven respondents not identified by village.

electorate in 1962. The rejection of the 1961 proposal meant that another year was added to the completion date of the second school. Between 1961 and 1962, New Trier's enrollment increased by 337, to a total of 4,513—1,013 over the designed maximum capacity of the facilities. By 1965, when the new school would open *if* the 1962 referendum were approved, the estimated enrollment would be 5,148. Between referenda, the educational consequences of delaying settlement of the expansion question were recognized as more costly than the issues involved. It appears likely that a shift in value ordering took place which significantly affected voting behavior in 1962. Objections to the location and cost of the second school site were overshadowed by serious community concern as to the consequences of overcrowded schoolrooms. Mobile classrooms were installed in 1962, and double shifts were anticipated before the new school was built. If this situation was not to worsen, the community that professed a desire to maintain New Trier's high standards had little choice but to approve the 1962 proposal despite the increased cost. Furthermore, New Trier's families, already residents of the highest-prestige community in the metropolitan area, could not escape the consequences of inaction by fleeing to a "better" district. The only alternative was to remain and solve the problem.

(b) *Multiple loyalties:* The second condition hypothesized for the viability of a plural community is the development of identification with, and loyalty to, the larger political system, in addition to established allegiance to the primary (municipal) unit. The definition of loyalty employed is Guetzkow's: "an attitude predisposing its holder to respond toward an idea, person or group, with behavior perceived by its holder to be supportive of . . . the continued existence of the object toward which the attitude is directed." [10]

Events preceding and immediately following the first site referendum suggest that the level of loyalty to the plural community may have been insufficient to generate the supportive behavior necessary to overcome the attachment to the primary unit. An alternative explanation is that the existence of multiple loyalties produced cross-pressures on the residents concerning the use of limited resources which were resolved in favor of the primary community. Northfield residents displayed a strong negative reaction to the proposal by plural community officials that additional educational facilities be located in their village; construction of these facilities, they argued, would be inimical to the best interests of the village regardless of the conceded value to the larger community. Similarly, when the village trustees of Winnetka (influenced by the negative vote of residents at the annual town meeting) rejected the proposal to use the "ideal" site owned by the village, their action was based largely on perceived future village needs, the needs of the plural community to the contrary notwithstanding. This position was buttressed by the

---

[10] Harold Guetzkow, *Multiple Loyalties: A Theoretical Approach to a Problem in International Organization* (Princeton: Center for Research on World Political Institutions, 1955), p. 8.

we-have-done-enough-for-New-Trier-already attitude prevalent among Winnetkans.

The results of both site referenda lend credence to the proposition that multiple loyalties, measured by supportive behavior (votes), develop more firmly in areas removed from what are perceived as negative consequences of plural-community decisions. Thus, in the 1961 referendum, both Northfield, where the new facility was to be located, and west Wilmette, which opposed the *de facto* social segregation that would ensue, rejected the School Board's proposal, while the eastern precincts, all of which would benefit from the plan without sharing in the disadvantages (i.e., overcrowding would be relieved in old New Trier by removing the primary cause—population growth in Northfield and west Wilmette), supported it. Similarly, in 1962, with the acceptance of the "major villages" districting policy by the Board of Education, only Northfield, the locus of the new school, and the Catholic population of west Wilmette had cause to refuse support of the plural community. (Given the high value attached to education in the District and the relative wealth of the community, the assumption throughout this analysis is that the cost of the referenda was not perceived as a disadvantage great enough to inhibit supportive behavior.)

The significant increase in supportive behavior in each of the District's precincts, including Northfield and west Wilmette, between the first and second referenda, suggests an increased identification with the plural community at the expense of village loyalty. This change might be explained in terms of perceived community crisis—i.e., what had been a controversy between east and west in 1961 was recognized by the entire New Trier community as a crisis in 1962. The transition from controversy to crisis developed with the immediate necessity for expanded facilities, as demonstrated by a representative group of community leaders (the Citizens' Study Committee) and the considered advice of technical experts in their respective fields—the Real Estate Research Corporation and Superintendent Cornog. This need, evident before the first referendum but inadequately communicated at that time by the Board of Education, was effectively transmitted in 1962 through the further use of experts—a committee of professional public relations executives. This strategy raised the cogency of the issue in 1962 to a level which elicited a significant increase in loyalty to, and support for, the plural community.[11]

(c) *An effective communications network:* The lack of effective communications between school officials and District voters was in large part responsible for the defeat of the 1961 referendum. The high value placed on conformity and nonconflict in the New Trier suburbs, as formalized in the caucus system of electing School Board members, made it virtually impossible for the Board of Education to anticipate the discontent that followed its 1961 expansion decision. Until 1960, the western section of the District was without representation on the Board of Education at all, and the election of a trustee from Northfield at that time still left a large area—including Glenview and west Wilmette—without an official channel for expressing its dissatisfaction. Prior to 1961 there were no effective means for conveying public sentiment to the educational decision makers, who traditionally paid little attention to public opinion anyhow, and who based their decisions instead on the judgment of an educational specialist, i.e., the superintendent. But the School Board's ill-fated attempt to communicate its intentions and rationale to the electorate in a series of public meetings before the 1961 referendum illustrated the ineffectiveness of the communications channels between decision makers and validators. The necessity for a "hard sell" campaign was novel to the Board,

[11] Even in the two precincts where the 1962 proposal failed, the proportion of affirmative votes was almost double that in 1961 (see Table 10). In Northfield, virtually all those who had led that village's opposition to the proposition in 1961 actively supported it in 1962.

whose previous decisions (with the exception of the 1957 referendum, recognized by the Board as a unique event) had been accepted without serious challenge. The public appearances of Board members on a village-by-village basis in 1961 served only to reinforce pre-established attitudes in specific communities without conveying the community-wide consequences of both the problem and the proposed solution. Furthermore, the only established district-wide communications media—the Hollister newspapers—remained unconvinced by the School Board's program and did not support it editorially. Nor did the Board make a serious effort to solicit Hollister support. Again, it was *assumed* that such support would be forthcoming without effort, as it had been in the past. Instead, the local press became a forum for the expression of views contrary to those of the Board, and for inter-village bickering. Such ineffective use by the protagonists of the available communications media, both mass and personal, was divisive rather than integrative.

The defeat of the first site referendum resulted in significant changes in the Board's attitude toward its constituency and in the means of communication between them. For the first time, the New Trier Board of Education attempted to increase the *sources* through which it received community opinion while it was in the process of making a major policy decision. Running scared, the trustees felt it necessary to determine what the public wanted. A group of civic leaders representing all sections of the plural community (the Citizens' Study Committee) was appointed to study the problem and advise the Board. This was clearly an attempt at co-optation,[12] intended to reduce polarization of community opinions. But it also served, whether so intended or not, to increase the number of access points for the expression of

[12] See Philip Selznick, *TVA and the Grass Roots* (Berkeley: University of California Press, 1949), and James S. Coleman, *Community Conflict* (Glencoe, Ill.: The Free Press, 1957), p. 17, for a discussion of the co-optation concept.

citizen dissatisfaction, which thus became a significant factor in the policy-making process.

The Board also used joint meetings with the District's elementary school district trustees and administrators to solicit opinions. And at regular New Trier Board meetings, for the first time opinions of citizens in attendance, the number of whom rose sharply after the defeat, were requested.

Perhaps more important in terms of the Board's objective—i.e., the integration of disparate community factions to such an extent that a public consensus could be reached on an educationally sound expansion alternative—was the use of intermediate *information transmitters*. Face-to-face interaction of the School Board and administration with the public was supplemented by community-wide communications media—some established, others created on an *ad hoc* basis. In both cases the use of plural community organizations with established *inter-village* communications networks served an integrative function. Information was transmitted from policy makers to electorate uniformly throughout the District, not by the policy makers themselves, but by local members of "overlapping organizations" supportive of the educational policy makers' program. The whole campaign was organized and conducted on an inter-village level, emphasizing the interdependence of the New Trier municipalities in a common cause. This process contrasted significantly with the School Board's single-handed attempt in 1961 to sell the program on a village-by-village basis; that strategy had stressed separateness rather than common interest.

Established community organizations used as transmitters in the 1962 campaign included the New Trier Parents' Association, the New Trier Township (school) Superintendents' Association, the New Trier High School student body, the joint committee of the township League of Women Voters organizations, and the Hollister papers. The Committee for Two New Triers was created by the Board specifically to serve as a centrally organized communications channel between it and the community.

The integrative function of the suburban communications systems in a plural community can be examined in terms of social organization and control. The physical separation of what Janowitz has termed the "residential community" and the "employment community" characterizes most suburbs.[13] The majority of suburban breadwinners work in the central city, spending only leisure time in the residential community, and find it difficult to keep themselves apprised of local events. Such difficulties are compounded by a suburb's involvement in a plural community divided by arbitrary political boundaries. The community communications system—social and civic organizations, and mass media—serves as a social mechanism to integrate employment and residential communities, and primary units within the plural community. These media are used to promote and maintain community consensus by creating images of themselves as nonpartisan agents of the community interest and by stressing the community's common values.[14]

In New Trier, the major communications channel for local information is the local newspaper chain operated by Lloyd Hollister. A recent survey indicates the extent to which residents used the papers to inform themselves about developments in the expansion problem. Of the 81 per cent who said they knew about the 1963 referendum, 76 per cent reported that they had gotten their information from the Hollister papers. Furthermore, as judged by the interviewers, 78 per cent of those questioned had complete information.[15] Results

[13] Morris Janowitz, *Community Press in an Urban Setting* (Glencoe, Ill.: The Free Press, 1952).

[14] *Ibid.*, pp. 73–74, 154.

[15] Data from a survey conducted by the A. C. Nielsen Company as a "public service" prior to the March, 1963, building referendum; the data, based on interviews with 223 residents, were published in the *Wilmette Life*, February 28, 1963.

from a study of Winnetka in 1960, in which 74 per cent of the respondents reported the Hollister press as the source of their information concerning community events, support this finding.[16]

. School leaders apparently recognized the influence of the local press, because publisher Hollister was asked to co-operate with the School Board in the second campaign. A strong New Trier booster, Hollister obliged by having a reporter present at every Board meeting and by giving New Trier expansion developments good coverage as well as editorial support. The importance of the local press in forming public opinion was apparent when, for seven months following the 1962 referendum approval, virtually nothing about the forthcoming building referendum was published, and the public became apprehensive. Word-of-mouth rumors filled the void and created confusion.

At least one student of local controversy contends that the newspapers' role in a community conflict is limited:

> In times of community dispute . . . the problem is what to *think*, how to make up one's mind. Because people depend on their friends and neighbors in matters of opinion . . . the mass media play a less important role.[17]

The Board established the Committee for Two New Triers to take advantage of this principle. Organized on a block-by-block basis so that neighbors talked to neighbors, the committee's campaign combined central control and dissemination of information with personal communication in conveying to District voters the seriousness of the problem and the efficacy of the Board's proposed solution. Question-and-answer booklets were prepared by a central committee of public relations experts, but block workers were made prima-

[16] *Social and Political Participation and Opinions in Winnetka* (mimeo.; Center for Metropolitan Studies, Northwestern University, Jan. 20, 1961), p. 11.

[17] Coleman, *Community Conflict*, p. 24.

rily responsible for getting out the "yes" vote, with each worker being assigned a very limited number of homes in his immediate neighborhood.

Personal communications also played a key role in reducing inter-village barriers. The formation of the Citizens' Study Committee allowed representatives from all six villages to exchange views and negotiate differences *before* the Board of Education declared new expansion policy. Several members of this committee remained actively involved in the campaign after the committee was disbanded. Their homes and offices became unofficial communications centers for the exchange of information among community leaders, including those opposed to the Board's proposal. One former CSC member reported spending four to five hours a day on the phone, making and receiving calls concerning the 1962 site referendum.

Efforts were also made to establish communications between the School Board and its opponents prior to the second referendum. Board members contacted opponents on several occasions to determine the basis of their objections and to attempt to convince them to withdraw their opposition. And on at least one occasion, Board members asked opposition leaders to withdraw an anti-referendum ad in the local press.

The combination of modes and levels of inter-village communications increased interest in the New Trier "problem" as a community-wide issue, and it also increased support for the solution proposed by the Board.

(d) *Cosmopolitan leadership:* In the analytic framework constructed for examining the integrative process among political units, one hypothesis stresses the importance of a plural-community leadership structure to bridge the barriers of primary-community identification and allegiance. Such leaders, who might be labeled "cosmopolites," are defined as those community actors who interpret situations and events in terms of their consequences for the plural community, and who have the power to influence community opinion and action. Their power may result from possession of a formal position of authority (i.e., a public office), from social status, or from special abilities or knowledge. In each of the three cases, the social control exercised by one individual or group over others is enhanced, through the compliant reception of the former's authority by the latter.

In a recent study of the political process in a homogeneous community, Holderman has concluded that where social, economic, and educational status (what Max Weber called "traditional authority," and what Holderman labels "rank authority") is widespread, community leadership tends to devolve upon persons or groups with special knowledge and skills, or what he terms "technical authority" (and Weber called "legal-rational authority").[18]

Certainly the voices which carry the most authority in the New Trier community belong to technical authorities, although the nominal leaders like to think they are in charge. The relative equality in social rank among New Trier residents, including those elected as school district trustees, considerably reduces whatever authority might be derived from official policy-making positions. The residents of the community, with the possible exception of new arrivals in west Willmette (who the established residents feel have not yet "earned" their status), consider themselves social equals, each capable of performing the tasks required of public office. Indeed, those who are elected school trustees do not view it as a position of prestige at all, but as a civic responsibility which they are expected to perform. Said one second-term Board member:

[18] James B. Holderman, *Decision-Making and Community Leadership in the Village of Winnetka, Illinois* (unpublished Ph.D. dissertation, Northwestern University, 1962), chs. i and iii; H. H. Gerth and C. Wright Mills (eds.), *From Max Weber: Essays in Sociology* (New York: Oxford University Press, 1958), pp. 294–96.

It's a position of respect; no one thinks less of you for it. They respect you for the time you devote to it. No one doubts an honest effort, or your motives or integrity. But no position in the District has prestige; there are too many people of high status in the community.[19]

And a past president of the Board commented that "the Board is worthy of the best individuals in the community—but they add to the Board's prestige, not the Board to theirs."[20]

The Board of Education's inability to achieve compliant reception of its decisions is also affected by the professional-managerial orientation of the District's population. In their own occupations, New Trier residents rely on experts and technicians to perform tasks and supply information in fields in which they themselves are not trained. They expect suburban government, including school districts, to operate in a similar manner. The citizens of New Trier want the best possible public service for their tax dollars, particularly when it involves the education of their children, and they feel the logical way to get it is to go to those specifically trained to do the job.

Furthermore, a significant portion of time is spent by Board members in their employment community, which for most is outside the residential community. Of the ten persons who served on the Board during the expansion controversy, eight worked in the central city (Chicago) and two (both wives of commuters) were actively involved in numerous community civic and social organizations. The time they could or would devote to school affairs was therefore limited. In fact, except for emergencies, the New Trier Board met no oftener than once a month. Under such circumstances, it was inevitable that both the community and the elected school officials came to rely on the hired experts that operated the

---

[19] Interview with Allen Stults (Wilmette), November 26, 1962.
[20] Interview with Marshall Long (Wilmette), December 3, 1962.

educational system on a day-to-day basis, and on others with special knowledge and skills to perform technical tasks.

This is not to say, however, that the resident community actors are without ability or motivation. Indeed, virtually every citizen considered for caucus endorsement as a New Trier trustee had had experience as an elementary district trustee or had been involved in the field of education in some other capacity. In addition, all were well-educated (none with less than a bachelor's degree and many with advanced degrees), long-term residents committed to the community and its welfare, and leaders in their professional fields. For instance, the 1963 Board was composed of two women who were North Shore civic leaders, a vice-president of the Inland Steel Corporation, the president of a large Chicago Loop bank, the president of Encyclopaedia Britannica, Inc., a senior partner in a large Loop law office, and a professor of business economics at Northwestern University.

The New Trier Citizen's Study Committee was composed of people prominent in local, midwestern, and national affairs, including the president of the Chicago Board of Trade, a former Democratic nominee for governor of Illinois, and the Comptroller of the United States, who resigned from the CSC to accept this appointment by President Kennedy. Top executives from some of the leading advertising and public relations firms in the country (all New Trier residents) were recruited to form the New Trier Information Committee.

Often, however, the level of commitment of these people to their employment community is higher than that to their residential community. As a result, they generally speak with more authority at work than they do at home. What community leadership is exhibited by the residents tends to come from those most involved in, most knowledgeable about, and most committed to the residential community. For example, the hardest workers on the CSC were not the "big names" but those whose status derived from local activities.[21]

Even the opposition leaders were those most involved in the local community. Mrs. Hall is a Winnetka housewife; Roy Pavlik, a Wilmette entrepreneur; Robert Sale, a Kenilworth civil engineer; and Jeremy Beman, an executive with A. C. Nielsen Company, a market research firm located on the boundary between Chicago and the North Shore suburbs.[22]

Thus a congeries of factors contributes to the fact that leadership in the New Trier plural community is largely exercised by professional "experts." The nominal leaders lack time, involvement in the community (particularly in the plural community), and the willingness to risk unpopular policy decisions in a community where rank authority is widespread. Perhaps more important, in terms of our interest in plural community leadership, is the absence of social and political mechanisms that would encourage an individual to become a "cosmopolite." Although the elected leaders all express the opinion that the idea of strict representation is abhorrent to the community—i.e., that it wants "seven responsible citizens" as trustees, regardless of the villages from which they come—by informal agreement the trustees are in fact elected as representatives of villages. The rationale for informal village representation is to create a communications channel between Board and village. One trustee viewed her role as follows:

[21] The chairman of the CSC admitted that the best work of that group was done by J. Stanley Blum, a Northfield businessman; Mrs. Alschuler, a Glencoe housewife; and Abraham Fell, who owns and operates a chain of clothing stores on the North Shore.

[22] For an analysis of the difference between the "locals" and the "cosmopolitans," see Gresham Sykes, "The Differential Distribution of Community Knowledge," in Hatt and Reiss (eds.), *Cities in Society* (revised; Glencoe, Ill.: The Free Press, 1959), pp. 711–21. Also see Alvin W. Gouldner, "Cosmopolitans and Locals: Toward an Analysis of Latent Social Roles," *Administrative Science Quarterly*, December, 1957, pp. 281–306 (Part I), and March, 1958, pp. 444–80 (Part II).

I take policy from the Board to Glencoe and interpret the needs of the Board to the village. My being on the Board brings Glencoe closer to New Trier. The people feel close to the elementary schools, but New Trier is bigger and more removed. Parents feel more remote since the Parents' Association is not too active. Having a village representative on the Board brings them closer to the high school and its problems. The pipeline is open for communication. The superintendent is too far removed from the people in a large district.[23]

But increasing the identification of single villages with the District through the use of *de facto* representative districts tends to decrease the responsibility of the trustees for the District as a whole, and makes it difficult for them to become true community-wide leaders, despite their professions to the contrary. This tendency is enhanced by the lack of competition for Board positions, which makes it unnecessary to weigh the opinions of the various villages and sections of the District. For instance, a recent president of the New Trier Board remarked:

Board members represent the entire District, almost disregarding individual village interests. But it is difficult to become aware of the attitudes of the "new people" in the District [i.e., in west Wilmette] because we have little or no social intercourse with them. They are not represented on the Board; I feel they must *earn* that privilege in the community.[24]

The elected trustees of educational systems traditionally have relied heavily on trained educators to initiate and administer the bulk of school policy, because the American ideology dictates that the educational process should be apolitical. A professionally trained superintendent, it is argued, will make decisions based on the relative educational merits of the alternatives rather than on political considerations. The latitude given a superintendent by a school board in the making of

[23] Interview with Mrs. Richard Alschuler (Glencoe), November 27, 1962.

[24] Interview with Marshall Long, December 3, 1962.

policy varies from system to system, depending on the social, economic, and political composition of the community. Still, in all cases the façade of school board control is maintained, because government, including school government, by popularly elected representatives is also a valued tenet of the American ideology.[25]

The leadership vacuum left by the formal authority structure in the New Trier community has been filled by technical authority. During the long tenure of Superintendent Gaffney, he was able to combine his educational training and knowledge with community dependence to centralize leadership and authority in the office of superintendent. Gaffney provided the leadership necessary to make New Trier a system of recognized excellence. His role was recognized by citizens and trustees alike and, as a result, authority within the system came to reside in the superintendent's office. Upon his retirement, the Board of Education conducted a nationwide search to find someone to play the same role in the system. But, for several reasons, William Cornog has not played the same role. First, the community's esteem and affection for Gaffney have not been fully transferred to his successor, although he is respected for his educational expertise. Second, the New Trier community has undergone significant social and demographic changes during Cornog's administration which have divided the community. And third, Cornog's administrative style differs from Gaffney's; he has not assumed the role of leader that Gaffney played, but rather has looked to the Board to perform its policy-making function as defined by the table of organization.

Nonetheless, Cornog's authority in purely educational policy choices is unchallenged, and indeed is enhanced by the increasing number of these that must be made. Cornog's

[25] The similarity here between the city manager–council relationship and that of the superintendent–board of education is obvious. See R. J. Snow, *Local Experts: Their Roles as Conflict Managers in Municipal and Educational Government* (unpublished Ph.D. dissertation, Northwestern University, 1966).

power in the system rests on the Board's reliance upon him to choose from among the educationally feasible alternatives in the process of declaring major policy goals. That is, he virtually determines which proposals shall be submitted to the voters for approval, and thus controls the agenda of community controversy for the educational system.[26] Cornog's professional opinion determined the Board's decision to seek approval of a proposal providing for a second four-year high school in the District, even though it was realized that this plan was likely to force a districting problem and divide the community. Politically, the wiser choice would have been a freshman or freshman-sophomore "feeder" school to alleviate the pressure on the facilities, and at the same time obviate the necessity for separate attendance areas. Community integration would have been enhanced by such a solution, since all the villages would have shared common facilities. But Cornog's experience dictated that this was an inferior educational solution, and the Board accepted his judgment. Similarly, Cornog's views on the location and design of the new school were influential in the making of decisions concerning those matters.

Unfortunately for the Board of Education, Cornog's authority in educational matters was insufficient to overcome the disintegration between east and west before the first referendum. The large "no" vote in that election was basically affective, and the rational appeals of the technical authority proved ineffectual. In addition, Cornog is not considered to be much of a politician, and he failed to persuade the community of the desirability of his proposal.

For the second referendum campaign, Superintendent Cornog shared the role of technical authority with other

---

[26] For a discussion of the power to *prevent* community policy conflicts from being aired publicly, see Peter Bachrach and Morton S. Baratz, "Two Faces of Power," *American Political Science Review*, LVI (December, 1962), 947–52.

experts called in to help promote the program. Cornog directed the 1962 referendum from behind the scenes, allowing the co-opted members of the Citizens' Study Committee, the Real Estate Research Corporation, and the professional public relations committee to convince the community of the necessity and educational value of a second four-year school. The CSC strongly endorsed the second referendum largely because the professional population study and the superintendent's expert opinion were accepted as authoritative evidence of need. Similarly, in the 1963 building referendum, the public overwhelmingly approved a proposal for a $9,000,000 second school, having been convinced on the basis of the collaboration between two professional groups—the New Trier educators and a nationally known architectural firm specializing in school construction. In both the successful referenda (1962 and 1963), the official policy makers (the New Trier School Board) played a nominal leadership role. In both, technical authority achieved the compliant reception of the plural community electorate.

New Trier is an amenities-oriented plural community whose residents can afford to, and expect to, live the good life unencumbered by social and political conflict. The acceptance of public policy decisions made by those possessing expertise in their respective areas of specialization helps to provide such a life for them.

# Selected Bibliography

## Books

Bloomberg, W., Jr., and Sunshine, Morris. *Suburban Power Structures and Public Education.* Syracuse: Syracuse University Press, 1963.

Bollens, John C. *Special District Governments in the United States.* Berkeley and Los Angeles: University of California Press, 1957.

Bush, C. R., and Deutschmann, P. J. *The Inter-relationships of Attitudes Toward Schools and the Voting Behavior in a School Bond Election.* Stanford: Stanford University Press, 1955.

Cahill, Robert C., and Hencley, Stephen P. (eds.). *The Politics of Education in the Local Community.* Danville, Illinois: Interstate Printers and Publishers, 1964.

Chandler, B. J., *et al.* (eds.). *Education in an Urban Society.* New York: Dodd, Mead and Co., 1962.

Coleman, James. *Community Conflict.* Glencoe: Free Press, 1957.

Conant, James B. *The American High School Today.* New York: McGraw-Hill, 1959.

————. *Slums and Suburbs.* New York: McGraw-Hill, 1962.

Deutsch, Karl W., Jacob, Philip E., Wheaton, William, Tuene, Henry, *et al. Political Integration: Interdisciplinary Research Inquiry.* Philadelphia: Lippincott, 1964.

Dobriner, William M. (ed.). *The Suburban Community.* New York: G. P. Putnam and Sons, 1958.

Douglass, Harlon P. *The Suburban Trend.* New York and London: The Century Co., 1925.

Friedrich, Carl J. (ed.). *Community.* New York: Liberal Arts Press, 1959.

Gordon, Albert Isaac. *Jews in Suburbia.* Boston: Beacon Press, 1959.

Graham, Grace. *The Public School and the American Community.* New York: Harper and Row, 1963.

Gross, Neal. *Who Runs Our Schools?* New York: John Wiley, 1958.

———, *et al. Explorations in Role Analysis.* New York: John Wiley, 1958.

Guetzkow, Harold. *Multiple Loyalties: Theoretical Approach to a Problem in International Relations.* Publication No. 4 of the Center for Research on World Political Institutions, Princeton University, Princeton, New Jersey, 1955.

Henry, Nelson, and Kerwin, J. G. *Schools and City Government: A Study of Schools and Municipalities in Cities of 50,000 or More Population.* Chicago: University of Chicago Press, 1938.

Janowitz, Morris. *Community Press in an Urban Setting.* Glencoe: Free Press, 1952.

Katz, Elihu, and Lazarsfeld, Paul. *Personal Influence.* Glencoe: Free Press, 1955.

Lonsdale, Richard C. *The School's Role in Metropolitan Development.* Syracuse: Syracuse University Press, 1960.

Maloney, Joseph. *"The Lonesome Train" in Levittown.* University, Alabama: Inter-University Case Program, 1958.

Martin, Roscoe. *Government and the Suburban School.* Syracuse: Syracuse University Press, 1962.

Menand, Louis, III. *Hanover Builds a High School.* University, Alabama: Inter-University Case Program, 1959.

National Commission on Professional Rights and Responsibilities of the National Education Association. *Levittown, New York: A Study of Leadership Problems in a Rapidly Developed Community.* Washington: National Education Association, 1962.

New Trier High School. *Fifty Years a'Growing.* Winnetka, Illinois, 1950.

Northeastern Illinois Metropolitan Area Planning Commission. *Suburban Factbook.* Chicago, 1962.

Seeley, John, *et al. Crestwood Heights: The Culture of Suburban Life.* New York: Basic Books, 1956.

Suttoff, J. *Local-Cosmopolitan Orientation and Participation in*

*School Affairs.* Chicago: University of Chicago Midwest Administration Center, 1960.

White, Alpheus L. *Local School Boards: Organization and Practices.* Washington: Office of Education, 1962.

Wood, Robert. *Suburbia: Its People and Their Politics.* Boston: Houghton Mifflin Co., 1958.

## Articles and Periodicals

Alford, R. R. "School District Reorganization and Community Integration," *Harvard Education Review*, 30, No. 4 (Fall, 1960), 350–71.

Alger, Chadwick F. "The External Bureaucracy in United States Foreign Affairs," *Administrative Science Quarterly*, 7, No. 1 (June, 1962), 50–78.

Barth, E. A. T. "Community Influence Systems: Structure and Change," *Social Forces*, 40 (October, 1961), 58–62.

Carter, R. F. "Voters and Their Schools," *National Education Association Journal*, 50 (March, 1961), 29–30.

Chandler, B. J. "School Administrator and the Power Structure," *American School Board Journal*, 136 (June, 1958), 29–30.

Coser, Lewis A. "The Termination of Conflict," *Journal of Conflict Resolution*, 5, No. 4 (December, 1961), 347–53.

Crane, W. "Politics of Education," *Education Forum*, 23 (January, 1959), 201.

Dye, T. R. "Metropolitan Integration by Bargaining Among Sub-areas," *American Behavioral Scientist*, 5, No. 9 (May, 1962), 11.

———, et al. "Differentiation and Co-operation in a Metropolitan Area," *Midwest Journal of Political Science*, 7 (May, 1963), 145–55.

Eliot, Thomas H. "Toward an Understanding of Public School Politics," *American Political Science Review*, 53 (December, 1959), 1032–51.

Fine, Benjamin. "Educational Problems in the Suburbs," in Dobriner (ed.), *The Suburban Community.* New York: Putnam, 1958, pp. 317–25.

Goldhammer, K. "Community Power Structure and School Board

Membership," *American School Board Journal*, 130 (March, 1955), 23–25.

Gouldner, A. W. "Cosmopolitans and Locals: Toward an Analysis of Latent Social Roles," *Administrative Science Quarterly*, 2 (December, 1957), 444–80.

Hamlin, H. M. "Organized Citizen Participation in the Public Schools," *Review of Educational Research*, 23 (October, 1953), 346–52.

Horton, J. E., and Thompson, W. E. "Powerlessness and Political Negativism: A Study of Defeated Local Referendums," *American Journal of Sociology*, 67, No. 5 (March, 1962), 485–93.

James, H. T. "Schools Are in Politics," *Nation's Schools*, 62 (October, 1958), 53–55.

Lieberson, S. "Suburbs and Ethnic Residential Patterns," *American Journal of Sociology*, 67, No. 6 (May, 1962), 673.

Mack, Ray, and Snyder, R. C. "Approaches to the Study of Social Conflict: Introduction by the Editors," *Journal of Conflict Resolution*, 1, No. 2 (June, 1957), 105–10.

Mantel, S. J. "Education in the Political Process," *Peabody Journal of Education*, 34 (July, 1956), 2–8.

Minar, David W. "Democracy in the Suburbs," *Northwestern Tri-Quarterly* (Fall, 1962), 23–28.

————. "School, Community, and Politics in Suburban Areas," in Chandler, B. J., *et al.* (eds.), *Education in an Urban Society*. New York: Dodd, Mead and Co., 1962, pp. 91–102.

Morlan, R. L. "Toward City-School District Rapprochement," *Public Administration Review*, 18 (1958), 113.

Moseley, E. Nicholas. "Politics and School Administration," in Hill, C. M. (ed.), *Educational Progress and School Administration*. New Haven, 1936.

*New Trier Newsletter*, New Trier Parents Association, New Trier Township High School, Winnetka, Illinois, 1957–63.

North, R. C., Koch, H. E., Jr., and Zinnes, D. A. "The Integrative Function of Conflict," *Journal of Conflict Resolution*, 4 (September, 1960), 355–74.

Ostrom, Vincent. "Education and Politics," *Social Forces Influencing American Education*, 60th yearbook, National Society for the Study of Education, Part II (1961), 8–45.

Rosenthal, Alan. "The Special Case of Public Education," in Frost, R. (ed.), *Cases in State and Local Government*. Englewood Cliffs: Prentice-Hall, 1961.

Seligman, Lester. "The Study of Political Leadership," in Eulau, *et al.* (eds.), *Political Behavior*. Glencoe: Free Press, 1956.

Shaplen, Robert. "Scarsdale's Battle of the Books," *Commentary*, 10 (December, 1950), 530–40.

Sykes, Gresham M. "The Differential Distribution of Community Knowledge," in Hatt, Paul K., and Reiss, Albert J., Jr. (eds.), *Cities and Society* (revised edition). Glencoe, Illinois: The Free Press, 1957, pp. 711–21.

*Wilmette* (Illinois) *Life*, January, 1925–August, 1963.

Zintgroff, P. "Bedroom Communities and the School," *Educational Leadership*, 17 (February, 1960), 292–97.

## Government Documents and Publications

State of Illinois, *Constitution*.

State of Illinois. Office of the Superintendent of Public Instruction, *The School Code of Illinois*, 1961.

U.S. Bureau of the Census. *United States Census of Population and Housing: 1960*. Census Tracts, Final Report, PHC (1)-26 (Washington: Government Printing Office, 1962).

## Unpublished Material

Brown, Wesley. "A Prediction of Maximum Enrollment After Building Saturation for New Trier Township High School District," November 10, 1960. Revised July 14, 1961. (Mimeographed.)

———, and Cornog, William H. "A Cursory Examination of the Several Proposals for Additional New Trier High School Building," December 15, 1960. (Mimeographed.)

Center for Metropolitan Studies. "Social and Political Participation and Opinions in Winnetka." A report prepared for the Village Council by the Center for Metropolitan Studies, Northwestern University, January 20, 1961. (Mimeographed.)

————. "The Winnetka Study," September, 1960. (Mimeographed.)

Citizens' Study Committee. "Report to the Board of Education of the New Trier Township High School District," Winnetka, Illinois, November 21, 1961. (Offset.)

Holderman, James B. "Decision-Making and Community Leadership in the Village of Winnetka, Illinois." Unpublished Ph.D. dissertation, Northwestern University, 1962.

The Leagues of Women Voters of Wilmette, Kenilworth, Winnetka, Glencoe and Glenview. "A Progress Report on the Study of New Trier Facilities," December, 1961. (Mimeographed.)

————. "A Report on the Study of Alternative Solutions for the Expansion of New Trier High School Facilities," January, 1962. (Mimeographed.)

Minar, David W. "Educational Decision-Making in Suburban Communities." Cooperative Research Project No. 2440, U.S. Office of Education, Department of Health, Education and Welfare, 1966.

New Trier High School. Minutes of the Meetings of the Board of Education, 1957–1963. (Typewritten.)

New Trier Information Committee. "Questions and Answers Relating to the Need for a Second New Trier Township High School," April, 1962. (Mimeographed.)

New Trier Information Committee. "Second New Trier High School Survey," May 7, 1962. (Mimeographed.)

Ostrom, Vincent. "School Board Politics in Los Angeles." University of California, Los Angeles, 1948.

Real Estate Research Corporation. "High School Enrollment Projections for New Trier Township High School," October, 1961. (Mimeographed.)

Rosenthal, Alan. "Community Leadership and Public School Politics: Two Case Studies." Unpublished dissertation, Princeton University, 1961.

"Rules for the New Trier Township High School Board Caucus," 1960, 1961, 1962, 1963. (Mimeographed.)

Snow, R. J. "Local Experts: Their Roles as Conflict Managers in Municipal and Educational Government." Unpublished

Ph.D. dissertation, Northwestern University, 1966.

Village of Glencoe. "The Caucus Plan for Selecting Candidates for Elective Office." (As amended to January 30, 1956.)

## Personal Interviews

Alschuler, Mrs. Richard H., member of the New Trier High School Board of Education, Glencoe, Illinois.

Beman, Jeremy C., Vice President, A. C. Nielsen Company, Northfield, Illinois.

Blum, J. Stanley, member of the New Trier Citizens' Study Committee, Glenview, Illinois.

Cappo, Joseph, reporter, Hollister Publishing Company, Wilmette, Illinois.

Farwell, Loring, member of the New Trier High School Board of Education, Northfield, Illinois.

Favor, Charles F., editor, *Wilmette Life*, Wilmette, Illinois.

Fowler, W. Raymond, Chairman, Committee for Two New Triers on a Wilmette Site, Winnetka, Illinois.

Gutzsell, Jane (Mrs. E. W.), Chairman, Joint League of Women Voters Committee to Study the New Trier Problem, Winnetka, Illinois.

Hall, Frances (Mrs. Herbert S.), New Trier Parents' Association, Winnetka, Illinois.

Harper, Robert, Executive Assistant to the New Trier High School Superintendent, Wilmette, Illinois.

Kerr, William, Business Manager and Vice President of Northwestern University, Evanston, Illinois.

Knoepple, Dr. L. J., Superintendent, Proviso Township High School District, Maywood, Illinois.

Liebenow, Robert, Chairman, New Trier Citizens' Study Committee, Wilmette, Illinois.

Long, Marshall, past President, New Trier High School Board of Education, Wilmette, Illinois.

Metcalf, Robert L., Superintendent, Bremen Community High School District, Midlothian, Illinois.

Misner, Dr. Paul, Superintendent, Glencoe School District, Glencoe, Illinois.

Pavlic, Roy D., Kenilworth, Illinois.

Sale, Robert C., Committee for Two New Triers on a Wilmette Site, Wilmette, Illinois.

Sprowl, Charles, President of New Trier High School Board of Education, Glencoe, Illinois.

Stults, Allen, member of the New Trier High School Board of Education, Wilmette, Illinois.

Tretbar, Everett, New Trier Information Committee, Winnetka, Illinois.

Weiss, Albert, Research Director, Chicago Anti-Defamation League of B'nai B'rith, Chicago, Illinois.

Wiltse, Dr. Earle W., Superintendent, Maine Township High School District, Park Ridge, Illinois.

# Index